Sales Techniques

"You can't just ask your customers to tell you what they want and try to please them. When you do, they will always ask you for something different."
(Steve Jobs)

1. The law of attraction

*"There are no magic or tricks that can bring you immediate success.
Success is achieved over time, with energy and a lot of determination".*

(Darren Rowse)

1.1 The most powerful law in the Universe.

Before pointing straight to the heart of our talk focused on Neuro Linguistic Programming and understanding some of the techniques aimed at Marketing, specifically professional sales, **I must remind you that there is a law of attraction.**
I have to do it not only because my morality requires it, but because it is good that you understand that **this law is the most powerful law in the Universe.**

I don't want to scare you and make you believe that after reading this book you will acquire a strange magical or supernatural power that will allow you to attract every potential client you want.
No. I just want to let you know that, if you take the existence of this law as good and start to go along with it, then everything will change radically and you will start to get excellent results both in work and private life. And I repeat, I'm not talking about magic and mystical and supernatural experiences (if you believe us then, the speech is different but I, at that point, don't come into play).

Now, you will surely be wondering what kind of attraction I am referring to (mental attraction? Physics? And so on, without mentioning an infinite list ...). And it is right that you ask. For this I will answer by trying to express myself as clearly as possible.

I am referring, therefore, at this moment to something far more complex, I am referring to the attraction in the broadest sense of the term, or rather to the pure ability to attract into our lives whatever we desire, whatever we address our (full) energy.

In fact, the law of attraction has the extraordinary power to create our reality in every single moment, to shape it, to improve it, to strengthen it day after day, moment by moment, moment by moment; for this reason, it is important to learn to exploit the great power of the mind to transform our thoughts into reality, to apply those communication strategies (in this case, in this book, we refer to all those communication strategies inherent to the sale, which we will adopt thanks to the knowledge of Neuro Linguistic Programming), rules useful to attract as many customers as possible to us.

I must remind you that there is a law of attraction and which is the most powerful law in the Universe.

1.2 The power of mind.

Attraction is the pure ability to draw into our lives whatever we desire, whatever we turn our energies towards.

Our mind is our greatest ally: in work, as in private life, having a clear mind, in stable equilibrium, allows you to face the most unlikely situations with fermazza; or at least gives you the chance to try. If we learn to create a perfect union between our mind (what we think, what we want, what we perceive) and our behavior and language (what we show in words and gestures, or the famous verbal and non-verbal communication of which we hear often talk) then, you're done.

At that point, we will be absolutely able to attract whatever we want into our lives, whatever we will turn our attention to and our energies. I know I might seem repetitive and, believe me, I would never want to bore you with this reading, but it will be necessary for me to repeat some sentences so that you can really make them your own. **So you can believe it. Because that's how it is.**
There are no magic or tricks that can lead you to immediate success - we know that well. The road to any kind of ambition is tortuous, difficult, fluctuating but the important thing is to never lose sight of the real goal for which we continue to move in this bureaucratic machine called society.

Whether you are (still) a mediocre seller or (already) a successful salesman you only have to continue to attract the best towards you, without stopping in front of the difficulties you encounter (and always encounter) in your career path. **You have to attract. Always.**

Success is achieved over time, with energy and a lot of determination. So, now focus on your desire for change, focus on your goals, focus on yourself and let yourself be captured for the moment by reading.

Before doing so, I would advise you to write down on a piece of paper what, in your opinion and in light of what your career has been up to now, are your weaknesses and your strengths. Writing down weaknesses first will allow you to take on a very human attitude (an essential component to any professional training. Remember: you are a man before you are a leader, and when you are a leader, envied by everyone, you will have to respect your employees by showing them your human component, as before and more than before).

After writing your weak points and having them read more than once, write next to (always using the same sheet) your strengths: these will be the fulcrum around which you will have to build, in the true sense of the word, your professional career.

Your strengths will help you make a difference in whatever sector you are acting or focusing on. And if you don't find them, because you are still a seller with little self-confidence and in search of his own personal and professional value, then choose a model that suits you and points to him! Write down his gestural and verbal strength and try to understand why you want to look like him. From this moment on, it will be an excellent reference point for you. You'll see, there will come a time when your image will look like you so much that you won't even need to remember it anymore.

It will be you. And you will always be the one to attract. Because you have to attract. And you will. You'll see.

The purpose of this book is usefulness and practicality: I will learn the main techniques of Neuro Linguistic Programming applicable to sales. Sales Techniques does not want to be anything else other than a useful and above all practical guide for you. I hope you will not find, in your opinion, anything extremely complex or convoluted. I will try to simplify, as much as possible, sentences and concepts so that you can fully understand them.

Yes. Because I am behind this book, ready to remind you that achieving success is possible and that it is nothing damn, absolutely, fucking, unattainable.

You just have to learn how to do, which communication strategies to apply, which behaviors to take in front of your potential client in all those different working circumstances in which you will find yourself attending.

So, let's start?

Our mind is our greatest ally and your strengths will help you make the
difference in any sector you are acting or turning your attention to.

2. The power of the Conviction

"Create your own style guide. That is unique and identifiable to others".
(Orson Welles)

2.1 Create your style, step by step.

I hope you have followed my advice to write down on the (famous) sheet of paper what are, for you, all your weaknesses and your strengths. Once this is done, it will be possible to transform those defects (or call them weaknesses) into merits because you will have a much clearer picture of yourself, of your professional figure and, before that, personal.

You will already know about yours, at that point, that you will have to work hard to smooth out all those corners of your character that actually prevent you from bringing benefits to your professional life (and before this private life) but, vice versa, only create disadvantages for you on disadvantages .
Of course, it cannot be changed overnight. This is why it takes so much effort and above all courage to undertake a similar path. But, from all this, it will be you and only you who will benefit from it. And nobody else!

You will see that the style you will adopt, and with which you will differentiate yourself from the rest, will be nothing but the final result of an important change process, in which your identity will be structured, as a whole, your strengths, and not of weakness.

Only through a real process of constant work on oneself can one aspire to become a true leader, but a leader who really makes the difference with respect to others, a leader with a unique and irreducible style, a leader who is always able to checkmate in the own professional sector.

You will have to learn to stand out from the crowd. You will begin to do so by sacrificing a model; you will grow to the point of overcoming it, with determination and a lot of willpower.

You know well, by now, that the ultimate goal of this book is to concretely aim at your professional growth. For this reason you will find listed here the best communication techniques and strategies that will make you an industry leader, charismatic and motivated, able to multiply sales, motivate his collaborators (and manage them above all), able to know how to communicate both in public and in private but, more importantly, you will be a leader who will make the used word a weapon to his advantage.

When I invited you to put your flaws and your strengths on white paper it was to encourage you to give a precise definition to some of the features that, in your opinion, best represent you. Let's say you identified yourself (negatively) using adjectives such as: anxious, talkative, nervous, agitated, you can be sure that you can't escape from these identifications! If you chose the adjective anxious and not the adjective friendly, there must have been a reason!

If you are (or have been) an anxious salesman, as you define yourself, it means that you have actually assumed attitudes, (in the eyes of your potential client or even just colleagues, for example), from typical performance anxiety.

Therefore, the time has come seriously to turn the page.

2.2 Not to forget ...

In case you have any doubts about what you've written so far, make a quick summary. It is important to stop and dedicate yourself (sometimes) to a review otherwise it will be difficult for you to memorize some of the themes that you will find in this book.

First of all, as a good seller, you need to know that each word has a precise meaning. And from that meaning one cannot escape. No turning back. If you appeared an anxious, pedantic salesman, you can be sure that that customer will never come back to you! After having a meeting with you, he will be left with comments like:

"What an anxiety this! From him, I will never go again!", "I didn't know how to get rid of it, but who is it? But how much do you talk about?", "But what do you want? Didn't you see that I wasn't interested?", "But how much he insisted? He no longer planted it! "," The next time I see him, I certainly change direction! ". If you are thinking that what you consider others about you, you care about the right, I'll tell you right now that you're making a big mistake! At least if you care about it, become a seller with a capital D.

You will have to be very careful about the identification they will give you! It sounds like bullshit but, in Italian grammar, adjectives make the difference, you know? You will therefore have to aim to exactly change these negative adjectives in their opposites.

If you call yourself a talkative salesman then, you must aim to be a moderately incisive seller, use to listen to and relate with the customer the fateful feeling of suffocation, and the desire to run like hell when you are in your presence. Creating the process of change also means transforming that: "I didn't know how to get rid of it, but who is it?" in a "The guy can do it, he's smart! Maybe he could really help me ...", "He inspires confidence", "He convinced me ...".

Create your style, and make it credible. To be credible you need to get the trust of the listener, and 99% of this trust you will get only if you are able to behave well, to show respect and to adopt a language appropriate to the situation in which you find yourself.

You must accept, before anything else, that there is no behavior that is split off from language! Your way of carrying, your attitudes, your behaviors are as important as the one that communicates verbally (and not, or facial expressions). **Remember => You are the result of what you say and what you do, this is the guide you need to**

create your own style.

There are no splits between the two, there can be no misconduct mixed with a suitable language, and vice versa. **Create your own style guide. And do it with conscience.**

Create a style guide that is unique and identifiable for others, but do it by adopting a perfect synergy between the behavior you assume and the language you use.

The style you will adopt, and with which you will differentiate yourself from the rest, will be nothing but the final result of an important process of change, in which your identity will be structured, as a whole, your strengths and not your weakness.

2.3 To make no more mistakes and time.

In the next paragraphs, we will talk about the word and the extraordinary power that resides in it. But now I want to reassure you. Because if you are reading this book you will be, in some way, prey to anxiety about the hypotheses of your future or, worse, you will be experiencing a condition of total discomfort on your current professional condition.

Perhaps, you will be scolded by saying phrases like: "I couldn't become anything I wanted to be", "I'm not a leader, I'm not fucking anything", "Because I insist on selling if I can't to do it? Perhaps it would be better if I gave myself to the horse ".

So, my dear friend, I tell you that you are completely off the track, that you are wrong to think so. Because **if you're flipping through these four pages it's because you're willing to improve and pursue the road to success that passes (necessarily, and I repeat it) through change.**
And is not the reading of this book the greatest indication of your

desire for change? Otherwise you wouldn't be sitting here reading me, I guarantee it. So you took the first step, and how you did it! So repeat to yourself that you have been good, that you have been brave and that you can do it.

I assure you that when you have finished your reading (you can also do it comfortably, don't be in a hurry, on the contrary! Every so often give yourself a break and make sure you understand the concepts so that you can then apply them in real life), something in you will have changed.

You will be a much more aware person and you will have an immense desire to try. Yes. To try to change, to experiment, to discover. And you will do it day by day. But until that moment, you will have to be a sponge to absorb all those concepts that may be new to you today.

Then I want to tell you another thing in a completely confidential way (that it remains between you and me only, in short). Who has never been wrong? To miss the way and the moment, for example. UFFFFF! To all (and here I would swear to be able to put the signature on the adverb surely).
And if there is one thing (most likely) that unites us all and our personal life experiences is the fact that, at least once in a lifetime, we have the wrong word. With our loved ones, with our colleagues, with our boyfriends. Already. We were wrong to use words appropriately, and we have hurt, or more simply we have lost opportunities that are important to us. We have the wrong way, time.

The phrase: "If I could go back I would not say more than ...", do you want me to believe that I never said it? Impossible. As banal as it may seem, either reductive, or simplistic, for what concerns my life experience I can tell you that life plays the rules of the here and now. Nothing more. And everyone has happened to make a mistake in the way and moment, losing the opportunity to enjoy that here and that time that could change an x condition.

Because from a simple here and now a next here and now is generated, and so on.

It looks like a puzzle, but it doesn't want to be. And it can be a here and now better than the previous here and now; always for the better. So pay attention to your here and your time: apply the best behavior and language you are capable of to your here and your present moment (your hour).
Remember => Way and moment, always.

2.4 If I pronounce a wrong word.

A wrong word in a certain work situation; a wrong word in a two-way relationship; a wrong word without if and without but. It is and will always remain a wrong word that probably did not go well. But when the omelette is done, what can you do? Try to roll up your sleeves and read this book!

If you don't trust yourself, you can also choose alternative solutions like meditating or going for yoga to relax your neuromuscular tension. But I could grant you this in a first phase of discomfort. Then no! Not anymore! A lost customer can become a fixation; a missed contract closure can turn into a damned worm in the head or, if you prefer, into a sweet and tender hamster that runs on the wheel that you yourself have placed in the head, exactly between your left and right brain hemisphere. And he runs, he runs wild, and you don't know where to start again (I thought, if you didn't like the hamsters you can always choose a crab that sails at the bottom of the sea, at the bottom of the SEAAAAA ").

Here it is.
Let's all calm down and you, instead, listen to me carefully: that word is gone, and nobody will give it back to you anymore. And you know what? If it was one of those potential customers for whom you would have made follies, by "you don't even know how many k of fortuitous euro was worth," know that you lost, because of that wrong word, a golden opportunity. We have established it. Now, fine.

Now, instead of crying over spilled milk, all you have to do is apply all the energies you have available and, I bet, you know you have (always after meditation, yoga and the journey to the end of the marrrr) studying this book .

To study. Yes. Study and learn not to harm yourself. You must constantly repeat this sentence in the morning as soon as you wake up and in the evening before you fall asleep: I will no longer damage you. I will know how to make the most of all the opportunities that will arise because I believe in it, because I want it, and because I can communicate.
Now, you have to learn to communicate to break through.
Kindly ask your hamster to get off the wheel and go for a ride somewhere else because, from this moment on, you will not have so much time left to dedicate to him.
Now you have to study, my dear.
Whether you want it or not.
And you have to remember life plays the rules of the here and now.

2.5 To grow it is necessary to study.

I, first of all, had to study. But studying so much, eh! And not just in books; I had to study books and experiences; studying myself, my behavior, my way of approaching the other, my gestural and verbal expressiveness.
I had to fully understand what was wrong with the communication relationship with customers, remembering the words with which I was harmed rather than taking advantage of myself.
It was a tough, indeed very hard job, and it is still in a completely experimental phase because, as I said before, you don't learn everything from evening to morning and, like any vice, you don't stop overnight.

Meanwhile learn that:

=> **Growth is professional.**
=> **Growth is individual.**

=> **Growth is continuous.**
=> **Growth is subjective.**
=> **Growth is in Farsi.**
=> **Growth is empirical.**
=> **Growth is important.**

Learning this (will it seem trivial to you?) Is very, very important to you.

2.6 The mind is your greatest ally.

How many times, just like me, you will have made mistakes that, thinking about it with hindsight, you could not predict brought so much damage to your company, to your own job, leading you, consequently, to believe to be a mediocre salesman / collaborator. One thing I want to tell you; know that if you are the first to think it (to be, in fact, a mediocre salesman / collaborator), then you will always be the first to damage yourself to the point of burrowing, burying yourself in this deplorable classification in which you made yourself fall.

The mind can be a great ally, but you have to give it a cheek. And you have to believe it, you first, in your goals and in your abilities otherwise you won't get any success; no sales, no collaborations, no realizations; nothing at all.

Apart from the fact that the causes of my / your / our / your / their lack of ability to communicate in a given working context may be of various nature, at this moment there is only one truth: if you are reading this book it is because you do not you are mediocre.
You are a leader and you do not know (not for long) how to be, how to become it.

I repeat (and I cried here): you are a leader because if you only had the interest to browse through these pages it means that you understood perfectly that your way of communicating is not sufficiently useful (for yourself and / or for your company) and that your work, at the moment, is not as rewarding as you would like it to be. You feel you can do more, you feel you want and can break through. But you can't.

You have understood that you have to go beyond your own limits, enter into a relationship with your listeners (in this case your target audience). In the meantime I can advise you to enter into a relationship with them on tiptoe: the ultimate goal must be to slip into their minds to avoid going out again (with the necessary precautions, of course) and this certainly cannot be done by assuming a impetuous attitude.
You want and you have to learn how to do it.

After these first few paragraphs, my friend, you know very well that:

• there is a law of attraction that can transform one's destiny through the power of the mind and you know that change can come from this awareness;
• each word has a precise meaning. And from that meaning one cannot escape. No turning back;
• you must accept, before anything else, that there is no behavior that is separated from the language;
• growth is professional. It is individual. It is continuous. It is subjective. It's in Farsi. It is empirical. It's important.

So all you have to do is continue reading to get into a free heart (as much as you can), in the world of Neuro Linguistic Pragrams applied to sales to learn all the strategies that this suggests, so that you can improve yourself professionally and find out how to get the maximum (for yourself) from your work and your life.

The study of some tips proposed by NLP you will need (daily) to support businessmen, leaders, just like you. Always remember, however, that at the end of the fair, despite the study of this lovely reading, only what you will be able to achieve will count, in other words, it will count what you will be able to take home.

If you do not bring anything (and I do not wish it) it will be only because YOU will not have been able to sell you well, to reach the other (the customer) on tiptoe; you will not have been able to read this book with the attention and care it deserves.

It will be only because YOU will not have been able to choose the beautiful words to use to attract and to convince.

3. THE WORD

"In the vocabulary the words are aligned, they stand on attention, they have a clean face. As soon as they become encrusted with reality, they break the lines and get rid of the squares in disorder: they loosen the belt and tie, show their tongue and get their hands dirty".
(Mario Postizzi)

3.1 The beautiful words to use.

Already. But what are these beautiful words? Some say that words can be a double-edged sword; in fact there are words that, if spoken in a specific context and at a precise moment (see the previous paragraph), have the ability to drastically change our working and personal position.

They can turn us upside down, make us fall into a confused state: "But I didn't mean this!", "It wasn't exactly what I wanted to say", "What will I have said wrong if not that ...", "Maybe I wasn't clear , I could have said that ... "," He still does not understand (he = client) what I am saying ".
Unfortunately no. Now that you begin to study Neuro Linguistic Programming you will understand how, in reality, in this trade you accept only an assertion: it is not the client who has not understood, you who have not explained yourself well.
This is another of the main rules of NLP to consider, always! And you have to remember it REALLY!

I regret you, always in case you missed some small details in the previous pages that, if you were wrong to talk talking to a papabile client, you missed an opportunity and, in 99% of the cases that occasion won't come back maaaaaai anymore! Now that occasion has gone to hell. And now it's clear to you.

If you said it, you said it; everything is already one step away from you and, assuming you don't have a relationship with this client (and I wish you no, because even here we would be sooooo to write), it is difficult for the other party to be willing to forgive you for using of a word called off-place or that is willing to give you a second chance (especially following your neurotic, confusing and / or intrusive explanation).

3.2 Come on, let's play a little.

> *"Everyone likes to buy but no one likes to suffer a sale".*
> *(Anonymous)*

With the customer you have to imagine playing a game.
To play, first of all, you must bring it to the same level. Never give the feeling of knowing more about him either in the field of your competence or in others (of his competence, for example). You and he are on the same level: the difference is that maybe he needs you (but he still doesn't know, or maybe he was starting to read up on your service or your product); you, instead, have a fucking need for him !.

So ... You always stand behind him and listen to what he needs. If understanding your needs may seem (at first) very difficult then you will be allowed to pretend to understand it (but only at first, I repeat), at least until you have become so good as to be able to perceive in full autonomy, from every single gesture or word, his needs, his expectations, his needs, his urgencies or even just those that are his simple curiosities.

It doesn't matter if you're faking, but it matters that you look confident in the way you express yourself and the way you behave.

The important thing is that, in that precise moment of conversation with him, you make yourself perceived interested in his requests; pretend (for good) to understand his words and value them, as if to say to him: "I am here now, it's all gone!" Later, when you learn to apply the techniques that NLP suggests to sales, you have already become a professional and, at that point, you will no longer need to pretend.

Play (not really dirty) but try it.

Call this game the game "Tell me what you offer and I'll tell you who you are." Remember that now you are on his own plane but it is he who moves the pawns, it is always he who will have to choose you, among many, after listening to you. I know, it's a bit of a strange game because it's like you're playing sitting on the bench, but it's nothing. This game starts the moment you get in touch with HIM.

And that's where, to win, you have to start playing.

You have come to Him. Here we are. You are going to put yourself at his same level. Done. Very well. You are facing each other. He turns the hourglass all at once. The countdown starts. You only have a few minutes to make him understand what you offer, what you went to do. Time passes quickly. Finished.

At that point he will have already created in his mind one or more ideas about you based on the perception that came from that meeting. All you have to do is wait to see if the damn card is green or red.

It won't take long to figure it out, trust me.

3.3 The words with a clean face.

Let's reread together:

"In the vocabulary the words are aligned, they stand on attention, they have a clean face. As soon as they become encrusted with reality, they break the lines and get rid of the squares in disorder: they loosen the belt and tie, show their tongue and get their hands dirty".

Beautiful quote, nothing to say. And I want to share it with you not because I want to be a slack philologist, this is certainly not the right time to be (although I have always had a strong inclination towards philology); if I chose to include it in this paragraph it is to push you, even more, to understand something that is much easier to understand than one can even imagine.

In the vocabulary the words are aligned, they stand at attention, they have a clean face - it means properly the words that we all know, that since childhood they taught us to express, first with sounds and then with letters of the alphabet , are perfectly aligned within our Vocabulary of the Italian language.

Someone before us has made the effort of the work by caring for us in our place. They are already there, one step away from us, well arranged. All lined up, like students in a row on their second day of school. Much of the work has already been done, so to speak.
So what should we do with these words? One thing is certain: we must not worry about embellishing them further (I repeat, Crusca has already thought of this years and years ago, indeed, Dante even before *Signora Crusca*). So our fortuitous task is reduced to knowing how to choose, accurately, nothing more!

You reproach me (surely) for how easy it is to say and little to do. I assure you that it is not so. But you will see it for yourself soon. So I confirm that it is easy to say but even easier to do, believe me.
Just don't get your hands dirty and be careful.

3.4 Let's not get our hands dirty!

Once you have learned from the study of NLP (applied to sales) what are the correct words to use and the appropriate behaviors to be taken before our carefully selected target, everything will be clear to you. These words and these behaviors enclose a finite whole and you will not have to do anything but draw from that whole with conscience, prudence and courage. Because we know, a bit of courage, in any kind of situation, never hurts.

I must know the words that are placed inside that finished set in order to succeed in this intent. Being prepared is an invincible method for not losing, so as not to make mistakes. If I know where I want to go, if I know what I want to bet on, if I know what I have to say in certain contexts and what not to say in others, if I know how important my gesture is for my profession, then my risk of failing is reduces and, consequently, my chance of winning increases.

Usually, it is not words that are in the power of men, but it is men who are in the power of words - wrote Hugo von Hofmannsthal (another aphorism that I love to quote). If you think about it, in a sentence like this we find the perfect summary of what we were telling ourselves (you and me) for almost half an hour. In the light of our speeches you will agree with me that we are precisely at the mercy of them, and not the other way around.

With the times in which we live and in the socio-cultural and political context in which we live, we find it hard to exploit the magnetic force of words, drawing them from their own beauty; instead, it ends up making an improper and ruthless use that traps even those who pronounce them.
But this has always been another story.

After reading this book and studying the main Neuro Linguistic Programming techniques, you will be able to apply (in full autonomy, I guarantee it) the correct linguistic behavior (verbal and non-verbal) in front of your customers; and not only!

If you have followed my advice so far (carefully) you will certainly have made (already) several steps forward, because knowledge is the first form of change. And you want to become a professional (and you know you want to be), otherwise you wouldn't have this book in your hands.

3.5 When a customer is not interested.

During your career you will be able to recognize on which occasions it will be appropriate to apply all the strategies that you have learned from the study of Neuro Linguistic Programming applied to sales and you will be able to understand (in absolute autonomy), at the same time and when you deem it appropriate, in which circumstance apply one of the most famous sayings in the world: silence is worth a thousand words. Yes, because in many cases, you will have to learn to recognize even when it is time to shut up!

"But how?" - you must be wondering, "a salesman can't just keep quiet, how could he ever sell? With the power of thought?" Now I do not want to say that it is truthful but trustworthy that, on many occasions, it will be better to be silent instead of speaking out of turn.

Imagine that the person in front of you has only 10 minutes to dedicate, not more; spent those sacred minutes will leave you in the lurch because he will have to run to do the shopping, and then take the daughter who goes to the nest (reluctantly), and then return and prepare dinner (always with the daughter of the nest in her arms) waiting that the husband returns, tired after a day's work, etc ...

Let's say that our potential customer, in this case a very simple family woman, gives you those famous 10 minutes of her life. In your opinion, what could be the best way to play it and take home the victory? Answer sincerely:

(a) attack her verbally by shooting everything you need to know about your product / service (inserting, here and there, clues to your personal life: "Hi, I'm Luca and I've been doing this for a lifetime, before I lived in Lourdes now I moved because our company .... / I, like you, didn't know about this product until I discovered it and now I can't do without it anymore, I recommended it to all my friends, to my family ... they also live in Lourdes, they didn't move. So, as I said, I live here recently but the passion for my work ... ";

(b) show a (fake) interest to his first: "No thanks, I'm not interested" by making you believe that you respect his position and then, a moment later, verbally attack him by shooting everything you need to know about your product / service (and so on) because YOU DON'T KNOW WHAT YOU'RE TELLING NO, YOU MUST KNOW IT AT ALL COSTS, HERE AND NOW;

(c) take an attitude that is as spontaneous as possible, inviting it, if it should discover its interest, to contact it again at that number which, kindly, you are leaving it attached to the catalog of your product / service. Because you, in the previous minutes, have explained to her why you could be useful to her and, immediately after, you showed respect for the reasons for her disinterest: you left her the space to talk and remaining to listen in silence.

Let's look at the answers you gave what consequences (work-related) you could get:

(a) if you behave like this number one seller (and I could mention it galore !!!), the immediate reaction of the woman is to escape. But the escape also understood as disappearance.
The next time he sees you, not only will he ignore you, but he will vanish camouflaging himself among the parked cars, quatta quatta, (he would be able to do it even with the little girl in his arms, you don't know what women are capable of in certain situations).

The end result will be that you will never, ever get from that family woman! Do you want to be an additional anxiety to her? Never be. He already has too many things to worry about, and meeting you would be an extra worry ... so, he'll stay away from you. If you have not yet understood it, you are anxious.

(b) In this case you will (immediately) be taken for a ride and will not give you a second chance. You deluded her. And women know, they must not deceive themselves. Did you make her believe you understood her, looked at her with an air of compassion, (perhaps more empathetic than compassionate) and then what did you do? You got screwed highly! You have been the egoist of all time, who has put his interests before you. Sometimes, at work, it works like in relationships, so watch how you move if you want to get away with it.

(c) If you have chosen this answer you have come close to the right solution and if you should, over time, convince yourself that you need yourself, your product / service will contact you. Because you were good at listening to it, you didn't worry about it like your other colleagues do; remember, however, that you need to bring home that contract closure, so staying silent can sometimes be very useful and can bring you many more advantages than you would get if you didn't, but also remember that here, I refer to the cases in the which the customer shows (immediately) a reluctant attitude or a clear lack of interest.

For this reason I suggest you aim for a range of users that you already know will be useful for you. Make a screen of your potential customers, aim for a precise targeting you need to save time and energy to invest in something else, such as a customer who will never be interested in what you do. And when you have a really interested client in front of you, assume the humble and intelligent attitude you know you can have by now.

3.6 Some examples of useless phrases to use.

I repeat again. If a customer is not interested in your service or your product it will be evident to you from the beginning so you will not have to in any way assume a damn persistent behavior by putting sentences / attitudes that create, in him, embarrassment and desire to escape.

Banish, from this moment on, all the phrases you usually use and that you think have a certain resemblance to the following that I offer you:

=> *"Look, trust me, what I offer you is unique, I guarantee you".*
=> *"I tried it and it works, since I bought it I immediately noticed a*

change".
=> "If I were you I would try it".
=> "Listen to me".
=> "Do you want to think about it? Eh ... look not to hurry but ...".
=> "We have only two more pieces for free and the request is high, so I would advise you not to think about it too long and take it now!"
=> "Take advantage, the offer is now, and it does not happen every day".

I'll explain why these sentence examples are to be banned:

• "Look, trust me, what I offer you is unique, I guarantee you".
The verb to trust implies a relationship of trust (literally: true faith, trusting) that at the moment, between you and the customer, it does not exist. You will first have to be credible in your eyes and then trustworthy. Saying this verb, in inappropriate contexts, is an attempt to indicate your need to burn the stages => so you get to him => so you get what you want. But this the customer warns him, and you will struggle much more to get his trust. Better to use verbs in reference to your service / product, (exalting the characteristics, the qualities, the benefits that it could get), but not to your person.

• "I tried it and it works, since I bought it I immediately noticed a change".
I have tried it and it works is the typical phrase that is heard by a salesman who tries them all to sell. This immediately creates an additional distance between you and the customer, helping to make you, in his eyes, a circus clown. He knows very well that you have not tried it and that you are trying to trick him or that you do not use it as you would have him believe. If it is true, instead of benefiting from it, do not say it, until such time as a bond of mutual respect has been created between you.

• "If I were you I would try it".
You are not her. You can't know what she needs right now. Yours is just an attempt at conviction that will lead to nothing, if you don't sell perfumes that you know, you try them more than willingly. At this point it is advisable to use phrases such as: "If you want to try it,

just ask ..." / "If you want to show them quickly" (very useful adverb in communication because it suggests your desire not to capture your customer by subtracting all the oxygen he needs to breathe, at least, until he has bought what you are offering him).

• "Listen to me".
Why should he do it? Assuming you're not the best in your industry, no one will feel authorized to do so. For this reason, I invite you to become the best and then show off phrases like that.

• "Do you want to think about it? Eh ... look not to hurry but ...".
Well no. You put him in a hurry and how. You understand very well that your intent is solely and exclusively to sell. If you are in a hurry, you will finish a little. Better phrases like "Think about it, if you prefer," which reassure and bring the distances between the parts closer together.

• "We have only two more pieces for free and the request is high, so I would advise you not to think about it too long and take it now!"
This sentence is a set of primordial errors that cannot be remedied. A mix between grip for bottoms, urgency to sell, lack of empathy and intrusiveness. I advise you to ban it completely.

• "Take advantage, the offer is now, and it does not happen every day".
Trust that if there is an offer, the first to know is the customer and if he knows it, and he is interested, he comes specifically to buy. If it hasn't done so yet, there will be a reason, so it's better not to insist.

At the moment I'm not interested can mean an infinite number of things. Probably, if I had taken a different attitude, he could also have revealed a fake or real interest: but not really! So I repeat to you that, in doing so, at the moment she will continue to not be interested.

Moreover, if it were by chance interested but the problem is that he cannot buy it (really) at that moment, you would create in him a feeling of inconvenient discomfort; in that case, it is better to inform the customer of the duration of the offer or other possible discounts, leaving him free to return when he deems it appropriate.

3.7 The Samaritan seller.

If there is a category of sellers that really gives me hives, it is that of the good Samaritan, or the one who follows you everywhere praising you as if you were a Greek God who came down to earth and doesn't let go of you for a while during the whole your journey you complete (if you can do it) in your store.

The 360 degree smile can understand it, those who hired you have expressly invited you to be courteous and kind and as long as you greet me, nothing to say. But if you continue to stare at me, even after greeting me, I begin to perceive a subtle form of tension; a voice starts to make room in my head ("Here we go again, this one will now stand with my breath on my neck", "But what does this ...", "Why don't you stop staring at me ...", phrases like that to begin with).

And what I am referring to is not a sporadic episode that happens by chance. Not at all! This is what happens most of the time if you enter a clothing store, for example. All personal experiences, I want to clarify; situations that I had the pleasure of experiencing personally and that I can boast of being able to tell you in this book.
This is the example of what I call: the Samaritan salesman, already.
Feel this (I always continue with the example of a salesman h at a store or clothing store).

To make you understand, I will tell you how merciless the pursuit can be for some Samaritan women. And I emphasize EXPLICIT! And I don't know of other useful adjectives that can make up for this identification.
Ruthless because they have no feelings, first of all; then why praise me for free when there's nothing to praise. And I know very well that there is absolutely nothing to praise.

If you suddenly pop up your head as a Samaritan salesman from under the tent of my dressing room (ah, how then do you allow yourself?), As if I were not even a Dinosaur Raptus survived the prehistoric ages, (ps = if you continue to emerge from below, I kicked back in one of those eras in the ass. And I also did the rhyme), and you tell me: "OHHHHHH, BUT HOW IT'S OK! from God !!! And then, what to say, it matches your light complexion and the blue eyes! ". Here I, as a common and deadly potential customer, put on my clothes and go away simply for the sake of spite.

And do you know why? Why do you make fake compliments to one who has entered your shop simply for the sake of amusing a little, after a hellish day of hard work, and came in there with dirty hair, sticky glasses and a milky white face - ghost.
And you had the barbarous courage to tell her that that color perfectly matched her beautiful complexion (I remind you of ghostly white ???), which made her eyes stand out (from behind two bottle-bottomed lights, explain to me how you got made to see them so bright or see the color ???).
But it's not over.

Not to mention the fact that you didn't allow me to try it that fantastic dress that I wanted so much because you, the Raptor Dinosaur that you are nothing else, you jumped from the bottom (precisely sticking your head from under the curtain) making me take a scare that not even I could describe you. Moral? I was left with my pants half-worn, a shoe yes and a no, and the fantastic dress that I wanted so squeezed across.

So ... Dear my Samaritan salesman or seller, if you are reading to me, have mercy on the customer who enters your dressing rooms and leave them free to feel as ugly as they like and like. And don't ask stupid questions after just three and a half seconds, "Come vaaaa ???" because I have the right to live, as much as you.
And to feel ugly, if I feel like it.

3.8 The pursuer seller.

Yes, there are many categories of sellers, this is certainly not the right place to list them; but I want to tell you another typology of sellers that I struggle to understand: the tracker.

We are always in a clothing and clothing store (I hope not the same otherwise you know what a mess).

They have no fault, someone taught them that to show an inordinate attention towards the customer is indispensable because everything is finalized to the purchase (or they threatened them with dismissal if they didn't do it, who knows , everything can be in this world of thieves).

And so those souls in pain, the wandering mines as I like to call them, chase you and chase you, chase after you and pursue you, they spy on you (as already said) from the slots of the door of the dressing room and if the slits are not there, then they they do it and then come back to spy you. And they pursue you again.

Probably of communication, they and the employers, understand very little; I would advise him to browse a book of Neuro Linguistic Programming applied to sales, to understand how to do it with many of their customers similar to me.

If you were your (poor customer) today, after such an attack, I would think twice about setting foot in this nice shop y. And it's not so absurd, if you think about it, that I've come to the point of telling you this with a certain conviction.

Because I, who have always been chased, whom I had to sweat to hide in the aisles of the shop and camouflage myself with pond green (even in the midst of the shelves of grandmother's woolen sweaters), I just wanted to take a simple look.

Exact. The only thing I wanted to do in that damn store was to look at myself in the mirror to understand what my hair was like (dirty, always as in the case reported in the paragraph of the Samaritan seller) before going to the supermarket and buying two packets of low-fat yogurt with coconut. Yes, I love looking at your mirror, so what?

And you, instead of letting me be in peace you chased me,

preventing me from looking at myself for as long as I wanted. And I don't know if I'll come back to you anymore. Because you'll always be there. Ready to aim at me from afar and sniff me as if I were a lost sheep in a pack of wolves.

It went wrong, though, because I understood your game and I'm not coming from you anymore.

And I don't care if they forced you to chase the poor sheep like me or if they just advised you, you created anxiety in me. And I will remember, next time.

And if you want to know, I'm not a herbivore. I know that you reader won't give a damn or a bullshit but I wanted to write it.

All this beautiful story, my dear friend, the future leader number one seller, I do it to remind you that how you move, what you will say in front of each of your individual customers will always make the difference. It is one of the indisputable truths on which Neuro Linguistic Programming is based.

For this you will have to commit yourself to reprogram your language, even before your mental patterns, because by improving your verbal and non-verbal attitude (your expressions), you will improve the reality around you.

Very probably you (and I hope so) you will become a rich and well-known salesman, a professional in the true sense of the term and, when this happens, you will certainly not remember the face of all those potential customers to whom you have imposed, in your own way to do, the ruthless escape.

But be careful! You will not remember their face, but they will always remember yours.

And if even for once you tried to trick them into convincing them to buy something that they didn't want at that moment, or simply couldn't buy, they'll have a hard time coming back to you.

This is the only form of punishment that they can afford for you, for having them so stressed. And trust that this opportunity won't let them escape for anything in the world.

So learn not to insist, learn from reading this book which verbs, phrases, words say in front of your clients, learn which gestures or behaviors to use; study and make the Neuro Linguistic Programming applied to sales; read and carefully review the passages in this book so that they are always clearer and easier to apply in the concrete of your work and private life.

Learn, thanks to Neuro Linguistic Programming, from your mistakes and find out how to apply the correct use of every word in every circumstance in which you will find yourself having to highlight your value, knowing that it can contain incredible power in itself and that, from this, you will be able to draw from it nothing but an immense advantage.

Whether you like it or not, you will have to learn to communicate and do it in the best possible way.
Always keep in mind, when you are about to take your very first step towards approaching the customer (always following the reading of this book), which is worth the saying: there is time and way! Always keep it in mind, but seriously.
In this book we will show you how to influence the client using a conscious choice of language, always after activating specific neurological reactions in him.

And remember that it is impossible not to communicate (this is one of the foundations on which Neuro Linguistic Programming is based today in the field of sales); I know that it is difficult to identify the correct words, intended in the sense of efficacy, and those to be avoided in order not to damage your image, but I will try to help you.

Aim to conquer your credibility on the market, as a leader that challenges business rules every day.
You have already started, now continue as well.

4. THE BASICS OF NLP

"What I do is to help people develop the conviction of being splendid people, because when you start to believe it, you also begin to behave accordingly: it is then that you begin to gather fantastic results".
(Bandler)

4.1 The Heart of Neuro Linguistic Programming.

You have arrived in this new world of NLP in which you will learn to make correct use of words and to develop all your linguistic and communication skills in order to achieve all those set goals. From the previous reading you know (now well) how important it is to take a positive attitude to attract to you the best that you wish to have.

Bandler, one of the founding fathers of Neuro Linguistic Programming, from the beginning in the field of experimental medicine supported (loudly) the importance of his own conviction, of his awareness, of his own value within every professional dynamic that aimed at change (and, why not, improvement).

The conviction of oneself (that is, the ability to believe that we can do it, that we can successfully achieve all our goals), leads us to assume positive attitudes. And only thanks to these can we obtain results.
From the results obtained it generates a very important element: Credibility. Without this there would be no change capable of leading us to the path of success.

But I want to go back to NLP, or rather to the heart of true NLP.

One of the fundamental bases of Neuro Linguistic Programming is based on a great certainty which is the following: all the negative answers that you have obtained (or that you will get in the future from your potential customers) will be nothing but the fruit of your wrong communication.

The Neuro Linguistic Programming reaffirms (since always) how much the power of the word is immense, extraordinary and the importance of the way in which this power is managed (first of all in the way we believe to be the most appropriate for us).

It is possible, and above all it is advisable to study the techniques of NLP applied to sales, to learn the most appropriate strategic communication method for you and / or for your company. Not all communication strategies are the same, you must always be able to implement (after having clearly chosen them) the best ones in your field of work.

Some of the greatest leaders prefer to apply marketing strategies based on the viral force of images rather than words. All right techniques, opportune contextualizing them for the purpose of a specific and personal success.

It is necessary, however, never to forget (and I want to clarify that I do not say this, but the story teaches everyone) that the strength of an image is far less than the driving force of a word.

Think of two hypotheses:

(a) in one we present ourselves in front of one of our potential customers bringing in hand a splendid catalog with all our products and our mythical / super offers. Proud of our advertising object, we wave it to the rooftops by showing off a brilliant smile but, knowingly or unknowingly (this can only be known by you), we take on an insistent attitude and / or use inappropriate words that will end up creating a hardship (not unimportant) and much , much, but so much embarrassment on the part of the customer towards us and / or the company.

(b) In the other hypothesis we suppose instead to have to deliver a catalog that does not properly reflect the classic graphic beauty (to put it this way) but we, aware of this, use all our linguistic potential to make that silly catalog cost only a few a real work of art. And that's where we learn to sell it; that's where we find out how to relate to the other part that, a few inches from our nose, listens to us.

Between the two, the greatest chance of success will be obtained following the second mode, and not the first. Warning! This does not want to ensure and certify the success of the second against the former, I simply want to say that, surely, there will be much more chance of this happening.

Obviously we talk about the ABC of Marketing and, specifically, about sales; it is obvious that in order to assert itself in the sector of our competence it is necessary to make sure that both hypotheses converge! We must use all those useful tools in order to obtain the maximum feedback from the customer: therefore excellent material, excellent behavior, excellent expressive skills, excellent product / service.

EXCELLENT LANGUAGE => EXCELLENT BEHAVIOR => EXCELLENT KNOWLEDGE => EXCELLENT EMPATHY => EXCELLENT MATERIALS I HAVE => EXCELLENCE OF THE PRODUCT / SERVICE I OFFER => QUALITY, CREDIBILITY, GUARANTEE.

To be more and more precise, we also say that the ability to communicate, to know how to sell (or sell a service, a product) is essential to make the sale an end in itself. Everything filters through our language, our attitude, our empathy towards HIM. Therefore, we learn to always pay extreme attention both to the way and when we choose to relate to each of our potential customers.

Based on what is supported by the Neuro Linguistic Programming the individual interacts in its totality through three distinct components:

- **the language;**
- **beliefs;**
- **physiology.**

The interaction between the three components mentioned above would allow man to create his perceptions (the perceptions of the reality in which he lives and of the world around him), giving these same perceptions certain characteristics, both qualitative and quantitative.
Thus the subjective interpretation of the individual would derive from this three-factor interaction; thanks to this structure (language + beliefs + physiology) he gives meaning to the world.

You will surely be wondering if it is possible to modify this trivalent structure, if it is possible that the perceptions, to which our interpretations of subjective reality follow, can be concretely modified. The answer given to us directly by NLP is, in this regard, absolutely positive.

It follows therefore that: we can modify, at any moment in which we desire it, meanings through a transformation of the perceptive structure (called map, that is the symbolic universe of reference); through this transformation every single person can undertake changes of attitude and behavior, of verbal and non-verbal language.

We come to the point, dear PNL, how can we change our subjective perception of the world?
Applying appropriate techniques of change and transformation that are in continuous evolution - is the answer.

In the first paragraphs we have amply focused on the importance they exert on us:

- the conviction ("What I do is help people develop the conviction of being splendid people, because when you start to believe it, you also begin to behave accordingly: it is then that you begin to gather fantastic results" - Bandler);

• optimism ("It is important to learn to exploit the great power of the mind to turn our thoughts into reality, being optimistic is the key to success");

• trust towards oneself, towards others, towards change ("You have to believe first in your goals and in your abilities, otherwise no success, no sales, no collaborations, no accomplishments, no nothing").

If I chose to focus a lot on these aspects, it is precisely because one of the main goals of NLP is to be able to develop successful habits / reactions by amplifying "facilitating" (ie effective) behaviors and decreasing "limiting" (ie unwanted) ones.

If embarking on the path of change in a first phase can be difficult, to the point of seeming almost impossible, (remember the exercise that I advised you to carry out from the first paragraph? If you haven't done it yet I would advise you to do so!), as suggested by the Neuro Linguistic Programming, the principle of imitation can be used.

That is, the founding fathers of NLP, we teach that the most profound change can also occur by reproducing ("modeling") precisely the behaviors of successful people in order to create a new "layer" of experience (a technique that can be precisely called modeling, or modeling).

Other people continually install beliefs that we end up believing in. These are the limitations imposed on you - wrote Bandler in an official paper about his working hypotheses, as he likes to define them.
In this quote from Bandler, which I remember being one of the two founding fathers of Neuro Linguistic Programming, one can easily trace (or summarize) to those that are the three components that characterize this discipline: Programming, Neuro, Linguistics.

Let's analyze them individually.

• Programming means the ability to influence variable behavioral patterns based on subjective and individual perception and experience. Through the use of some techniques of Neuro Linguistic Programming we would intervene on a predefined range of behaviors (programs or schemes), which work in an unconscious and automatic way.

• Neuro is the set of individual neurological processes of human behavior, based on how the nervous system receives stimuli from the sense organs and re-elaborates them as perceptions and representations.

• Linguistics, finally, defines the system by which human mental processes are coded, organized and transformed through language.

The Neuro Linguistic Programming is considered today as a discipline capable of bringing together the various fields of the study of human communication, proposing itself as a tool able to influence multiple factors, such as education, learning, negotiation, sales, leadership, team-building.
It has now found application in various garments, even in decision-making, creative processes, art, sport and counseling. The role he currently plays is very different from his beginnings, as we will see shortly: in Italy it began to spread in the early eighties, initially in the field of management training.

NLP is proposed as a methodology for studying the structure of subjective experience - writes Robert Dilts. According to the scholar, in fact, the practical goal of Neuro Linguistic Programming has always been to understand how some people manage to get certain results (I repeat that this, for NLP, should be done through analysis, learning and modeling , ie the voluntary acquisition of certain behaviors); to analyze this it was necessary to study the structure of subjective experience beyond which, vice versa, it would have been impossible to implement (in the subjects involved) any form of change.

NLP is still considered a pseudoscience, and the same supporters claim that its applications do not necessarily have to have a scientific basis, because the fundamental principles around which the Neuro Linguistic Programming is structured are simple "working hypotheses, which can be true or not "The problem is not whether they are true, but whether they are useful." It is extremely important that they be useful, because they must lead to an understanding of the subjective interpretation of reality; if there is no understanding of the self and of what is necessary to change, there can be no positive change.

The work analyzes formulated by the Neuro Linguistic Programming should lead, or at least be useful, to the elaboration of a behavioral model that should be (later) replicated by the "patient" through the acquisition of the models considered effective. To the acquired models (the models so to speak external from the subject that interprets) then, during the path of change, those models already in possession of the "patient", or those obtained from the positive previous experiences that belong to his past.

To best program your mind by applying the techniques recommended by Neuro Linguistic Programming it is first of all important to learn about the secret language of the mind itself. The mind is our best ally (see previous paragraph).

We have written it extensively over and over again the acronym PNL which literally means Neuro-linguistic Programming. This definition, desired by the two founding fathers Richard Bandler and John Grinder (known to be respectively a computer scientist and a linguist the other), cannot (certainly) be considered random.

I refer to their definitions (published over time) according to which the acronym PNL condenses the three essential principles of the neuro-linguistic programming system:

• The brain ("neuro") is to be considered programmable and reprogrammable (hence the choice of the term "programming").
• The brain ("neuro") knows and interprets reality through language (hence the choice of the term "linguistics").
• The brain ("neuro") is programmable ("programming") through

language ("linguistics").

So far, I have tried to explain to you what is the heart of the whole Neuro Linguistic Programming system, which principles it refers to (later we will briefly mention the historical context in which it developed) and why it is important, in order to implement a any professional and individual transformation, following which it will be possible for you to derive real and concrete benefits.

"Beliefs determine actions. The actions determine the results you get and the results determine the beliefs you create "- always. And then if these beliefs are wrong, then we are led to take wrong actions which, in turn, will only cause invalidating results for us and / or for our company, which will lead us to the creation of harmful beliefs, etc. .. It's all a big wheel from which it is difficult to descend, like a dog that tries to bite its tail.

Relying on the knowledge of Neuro Linguistic Programming techniques and applying them to the sales field means being able to use the communication processes of the brain (more precisely of the mind - brain) to modify them, reprogram them with the language itself.

4.2 Change is feasible.

"True spirituality means realizing that when you vibrate with real joy, people around you begin to do the same".
(Bandler)

When reference is made to Neuro Linguistic Programming, the concept of Map and Territory is also used. We must keep in mind that NLP does not specifically concern the psychic contents or the psychic motives that push man to assume a given behavior, but affect psychic processes.

I give a concrete example as a subject and interpreter of my reality. Knowing that I have developed, over time, a poor ability to show affection by blaming my family ("If I am like this it is only because my mother never gave me a compliment ...", "I don't know what it means to say I want you well because no one has ever said it to me ", etc.), it will certainly not lead to the solution of the problem: which in this specific case concerns the problem of anaffectivity.

Going in search of the motivations and causes that have generated the problem of anapectivity to solve it starting from its root, means to be interested in the psychic motif, and this is certainly not what the Neuro Linguistic Programming deals with.

NLP is concerned with the process by which I, as a subject, arrive at formulating my hypotheses; the way in which I am able to live my experiences (that is the way in which I manage to arrive at the subjective knowledge of the world, its interpretation).

Let us assume that over the course of my life I have developed an empirical awareness formed on the basis of my great affectivity; in other words: let's say that my interpretation of the world was forged on the basis of my lack of emotion. It is obvious that if I had been a passionate person my subjective interpretation of reality would have been far different.

Good. All these processes through which I, subject, arrive to formulate my hypotheses take place through language (I refer to not only rational language but to that better known as intra-psychic language: images, voices, sounds, sensations, emotional references, and so on).

Let's take another practical example. I am an anaffective salesman, indeed, absolutely anaffective, in my private life. This condition has conditioned my existence but has created such processes that I have the vision I have of the world today. Now. Nothing wrong with wishing to continue living a life by lying down in this condition of an affectivity.

But if I, on the other hand, suffer from this condition of mine that leads me to assume wrong attitudes (both in public and in private), harmful to me and to those around me ("how I will do it, doing so by being empathetic with my client ? ") then I can do nothing but decide to make a change.

And to know that this change is feasible.

To transform my condition what should I do? To reprogram my brain I have to start by reprogramming my language through which I communicate my experience of the world to myself.

Exactly. We must change language if we want to make a change and reprogram our brain. We think. If until now, as a good salesman I was, I used to run into a customer with x characteristics to which I replied (rudely) in the same way, (because my character, my life experience had led me to be a grumpy person), then I will not have to do anything but start to see that usual situation from a different perspective and communicate it, using a different language, an appropriate language, which will do me justice.

I live by creating experiences; the way I tell it to me will make the substantial difference from now on. The same goes for you. This is what you have to memorize carefully.

You can only get rid of your mental patterns later and reprogram the so-called paradigms you have built (or have been inculcated into) but, first, you have to start by reprogramming your language through which you communicate to yourself your own experience of the world.

There is no objective reality; it is impossible for you to find a neutral reality outside. It is only within us that our ideas are formed, that our interpretations come to life and our experience is permeated, filtered, by this continuous movement of subjective reality that is stirred within us.

Every day we communicate something or better we tend to explain our perception of reality; my experience is always an interpretation. Now that I know, I can intervene. I can change the language with which I used to communicate my reality to myself, to improve, to become what I always wanted to be, to tell me what I really want to tell myself.

Here, in doing so, we will begin to tend towards (RI -) Neuro Linguistic Programming.

After these interesting explanations a doubt might arise then, which will push you to formulate questions such as the following: just as the experience of reality is always subjective, at this point, even the language I use to experience reality should not be, similarly, subjective? Shouldn't it change from individual to individual?

And yet ... If everyone uses their own language, how can criteria be established that are valid for everyone? What do we call Maps, are they universal?

According to the results of the work done by the two founding fathers of PNL, Bandler and Grinder, we know that yes, we all communicate in the same way, that is we all communicate using the same language, the same linguistic structures.

But Neuro Linguistic Programming constantly deals with developing (and methodically refining) the understanding of all those linguistic patterns through which we not only communicate, but understand and experience reality.

Knowing how to use NLP (in this case in the field of sales) and be aware of its techniques, means knowing these linguistic patterns and knowing how to apply them daily, in front of every single professional situation or not.

What does the Neuro Linguistic Programming offer that other disciplines are unable to offer you? It offers you the real possibility of reprogramming your mind to live better.

4.3 A brief historical reference to the birth of NLP.

"We do not lose sight of the most important factors for success: commitment, passion to make a difference, vision to anticipate changes and courage to get things moving".
(Larraine Matusak)

Now that you have learned, in more detail, of the three principles of Neuro Linguistic Programming, which are the fulcrum around which the whole system stands, you can start to successfully reprogram your brain, your mind and yours professional life.

You have learned that:

• *Change is feasible, real and concrete.*

• *NLP offers you the real possibility of reprogramming your mind to live better.*

• *To reprogram my brain I have to start by reprogramming my language through which I communicate my experience of the world to myself.*

• *NLP is concerned with the process by which I, as a subject, come to formulate my hypotheses; the way in which I am able to live my experiences (that is, the way in which I manage to arrive at the subjective knowledge of the world, its interpretation.*

• *That I can intervene. I can change the language with which I used to communicate my reality to myself, to improve, to become what I always wanted to be, to tell me what I really want to tell myself.*

The Neuro Linguistic Programming is the result of an idea that has developed since the meeting of two brilliant minds (John Grinder and Richard Bandler) and destined to sprout, over the years, because it has found more and more fertile ground in which take root.
Today, NLP continues to bear fruit and provides us with all the tools necessary for reprogramming our mind, for better life, whenever we wish.

There is always time, if you really want to, to learn to apply the communication strategies of NLP, the important thing is the awareness of being able to change (as we have repeated many times): we can change.
It is obvious that the quality of the result will depend on one's ability. Making the change happen is an operation that certainly takes time; the fact remains that, the more you know yourself (the more you know your strengths and your faults), the more you learn about it (you learn to understand what's wrong with your way of bringing you to the customer, what's wrong with your way of

communicating, analyzing which are the disadvantageous attitudes for you and for your career) and you use the tools of PNL, the more you will become skilled; in short, in the end you will become a true professional.

For the most curious, I am now inserting a small historical reference to the moment in which the Neuro Linguistic Programming was born. Take it as a simple and optional in-depth reading, nothing more. If you are not interested, just skip it and go further.

It was the year 1970 when the newly graduated at the University of Santa Cruz in California, Richard Bandler, and one of the professors of that same University, John Grinder, decided by mutual agreement to start studying the characteristics of communication which, in those years, it was used by some of the best known psychotherapists of the time who dominated the internal medical landscape.

The two were strongly attracted to a specific type of communication, one that was able to produce real changes in the individual, contributing to bring him, also, remarkable healings. Richard Bandler and John Grinder therefore aimed at a communication that resolved effectively and with a certain marked continuity, as the two publicly declared.

On the basis of their fortuitous encounter, their conjectures and their working hypotheses, the two gave life to Neuro Linguistic Programming, defining it as an extremely effective method of communication and aimed at a concrete improvement of one's personal life; a system of life coaching, self help and counseling intended by the two founding fathers as an approach to communication, personal development and psychotherapy.

During their continuous research, Bandler and Grinder began to observe, in particular, the modus operandi of three great therapists. They knew and attended, first of all, Fritz Perls (Gestalt therapist) in the Esalen Center in California.

After analyzing the working method of Perls, the two began to approach the method of communication promoted by Virginia Satir, a smart and well-trained doctor in family therapy.

The two were certainly more attracted to the Satir model, of which they appreciated the great capacity of empathy, compared to that of Perls; thus, the peculiar therapeutic style of Satir led, both Grinder and Bandler, to pay great attention to the language she used during her work sessions and from which, subsequently, many of their linguistic models came to refer.

At the same time the anthropologist Gregory Bateson advised Bandler, who was a great friend of his, to also analyze the work of Milton H. Erickson, a very famous doctor at that time; Erikson was known to be one of the leading experts on clinical hypnosis.
Also from the meeting with Erickson extraordinary communication models were extracted which, from a certain moment onwards, Grinder and Bandler began to repropose in psychotherapy.

From the imitation (or modeling) of these three great therapists: Perls, Satir and Erikson, Grinder and Bandler came to the publication of two very important books that marked their respective careers: "The structure of Magic" and "The models of the hypnotic technique of Milton H. Erickson "(published in Italy by Astrolabio).

Towards the end of the 1970s, a (particularly brilliant) student of Bandler, Robert Dilts, with the collaboration of the master began to develop some useful techniques to improve the theory on Neuro Linguistic Programming.
Dilts is known today as the one who first approached the Neuro Linguistic Programming in a scientific way, starting to develop it and to always proceed in this direction. Even today, Dilts' work on research and development on NLP is very famous, ranging from business applications to the treatment of diseases considered incurable.

After the first decade the spread of Neuro Linguistic Programming grew considerably thanks to the further publication of three very important books (Italian edition: Astrolabio): "The Therapeutic

Metamorphosis", "Hypnosis and Transformation", "Restructuring".
Numerous researchers joined the studies of Grinder and Bandler and
contributed by providing additional information or presenting new
work hypotheses; and their help was, at that time, more than
considerable. Among these researchers we mention Leslie Cameron
Bandler, David Gordon (known author of the book "Metaphors
Therapeutics"), Stephen Gilligan.

In the mid-1980s a promising young Anthony Robbins took part in
the Neuro Linguistic Programming courses of Bandler and Grinder
because he had captured the great importance and the extraordinary
nature of the method. At the age of 24, Robbins wrote the book
"How to get the best out of himself and others" (published in Italy by
Bompiani) which later became a world best selller. "How to get the
best from yourself and others" was a book that helped to spread
Neuro Linguistic Programming and make it accessible to everyone.

In addition to the publication of the book, Robbins disclosed the
P.N.L. taking courses (increasingly numerous) attended by
thousands of people from all over the world. At the same time
Richard Bandler suddenly became the reference point (on a global
scale) of the specialization courses in Neuro Linguistic Programming
that are increasingly accessible to the public.

From a certain moment on, John Grinder withdrew from his
academic career with the aim of devoting himself mainly to training
in large companies. A short time later, Dilts moved to the University
of Santa Cruz; the Andreas moved to Colorado.

Tad James was one of Bandler's last students who had published the
description of some interesting techniques in a book entitled "Time
Line" (Ed. Astrolabio); a short time later, he detached himself from
Bandler to move and work in Hawaii.

Currently, the research continues in the field of Neuro Linguistic
Programming continues thanks to the work of Bandler, Grinder,
Dilts and many trainers who continue to enjoy considerable success
today.
Richard Bandler continues his work supported by John La Valle, an

extraordinary trainer and consultant specialized in the most advanced applications of NLP to business and persuasion, (co-author, with Bandler, of the book Persuasion Engineering, ed. Nlp Italy).

Bandler continues his work and recently, developing studies on submodality, he created the techniques called DHE (Design Human Engineering). Together with his composer friend Denver Clay he recorded a series of CDs that are the result of the combination of linguistic models with music and sounds, called Neuro-Sonics.
Only a short time ago, Bandler presented his latest work entitled NHR (Neuro Hypnotic Repatterning) that is, a set of methodologies mainly based on the use of sophisticated linguistic models to quickly induce change in the individual.

As we have seen, the applications of Neuro Linguistic Programming are increasingly widening or moving, quickly, towards new fields (from psychotherapy to effective communication, from rapid learning to sales and business, from communication in public to leadership, from performance sports to psycho-physical well-being up to the health field).

We can conclude this paragraph by confirming that, NLP basing itself on the principle of "modeling" (of imitation) of extraordinary people is surely, today, the most avant-garde science that exists since it offers models, strategies, resources and techniques usable by anyone (and I stress anyone) intends to improve (really) his life.

4.4 Bandler, a bit of life coaching does not hurt.

"Today you make a decision that you have always postponed, and tomorrow you do the same thing. You will train the muscle that can help you change your whole life."
(Alfred A. Montpart)

In recent years I have read some of the books written by Richard Bandler.

To be honest, in addition to verli beds I have also studied them, in the sense of having made sure to memorize those that were, in my opinion, the most significant motivational phrases.

With time we know, memory falters, I could not quote them here without first taking them back in hand; but I'm sure the concepts, oh yes, those, I could repeat them instantly.

I remember approaching Bendler because, at an important time in my life, the need to change had been revealed to me. I tried with meditation, with yoga, with psychoanalysis, with sporting activity; I also happened to mix things up, in some cases.

The result was a complex set of intersections between them. In short, a great confusion, thinking about it now. I tried to recover, in all possible ways, self-confidence, positivity, the courage that would have led me to change, to let go to "become" and go "beyond".

I knew well that many of the attitudes I assumed and the ways of speaking with which I confronted myself with the other person were the result of what I had convinced myself to be, up to that moment. I had built my reality by constantly filtering it with my subjective interpretations. I was doing damage, (said clearly and in plain English), alone because I was convinced that that way of speaking, of relating, of doing (based on what was my story) was the only way I was capable of. And I was really wrong. If I had known that, reprogramming my mind, and before that my language, I would have started living again, I probably would never have believed it.

They talked to me about reprogramming mental patterns, language, paradigms, specifically about Neuro Linguistic Programming and I was immediately kidnapped by it. I approached, for these reasons, NLP in a more than conscious way, and tried to change.

Not that it was a simple process, indeed. But it is necessary. And this necessity has allowed me to implement a real, concrete, feasible process for me (as it could be for anyone else). Just be willing to get involved and deal with yourself, and trust that this is undoubtedly the most difficult part.

I chose to include some of Bandler's most beautiful phrases in this book and they struck me most, hoping they have the same effect on you as you are reading right now; his sentences and his aphorisms about mental maps and mental reprogramming, linguistic seen from a much more human point of view, Bandler's point of view.

If you read them with the attention they deserve, they will be able to guide you on the professional path that you decide to take.

I have repeatedly stressed the importance of the role of Bandler (from the point of view of Neuro Linguistic Programming) and the resonance of his writings within the marketing landscape applied to sales.

But who is Richard Bandley?

Richard Wayne Bandler was born February 24, 1950 (Jersey City).

He is a psychologist, an essayist, a linguist, an American counselor and life coach of the best in the world. He dedicated his entire life to teaching and essay writing. Much of Bandler's work on NLP concerns the applications of submodality, that is, of the subtle distinctions that exist in personal sensory experiences and their internal representations.

His past as a musician and his interest in the neurological impact of sound led him to develop the area of the neurosonic, a discipline that uses music and sound to create specific inner states.

Today, among his best-known books we find: "Using the brain to change", "Guide for the expert on submodality", "NLP is freedom", "Live the life you want with NLP", "The power of unconscious and NLP ".

4.5 Aphorisms by Bandler, and much more ...

"You need the objectivity that allows you to forget about everything you've heard before to complete a study exactly as a scientist would do."
(Steve Wozniak)

We have entered the heart of Neuro Linguistic Programming applied to sales.

We have fully understood its meaning and it has been necessary to take a step back, signaling some historical-cultural element in reference to the context in which the NLP originated.

We have said that there is a law of attraction that originates in one's mental strength, the same that allows us to attract to ourselves all that we desire, if only we really believe in it.

We have specified however also that, to do it, it is not enough to believe it; we need some tools to achieve our goals and, in order not to get lost in the ocean of this research, we necessarily need a method that shows us the right path to take.

It will be up to us alone to choose whether to pursue that of good and that of evil.

The road to good, in this case, indicates the correct behavior to take in the presence of our customers, the right words to use, the ability we have to exploit the moment based on the predisposition that we are able to perceive of the other.

Here, the path of good allows us to achieve exactly this: the ability to anticipate the desire of those who listen to us, to understand what they really want (to ask ourselves if our service is effective for him, if we can satisfy him, if it is us who is looking for really).

Once the answers are all affirmative, then from the idea, which anticipates our process of change, we will move to action focusing on the linguistic and behavioral sphere.

We have seen how to make a single word wrong or take a wrong attitude is harmful to our profession. When a seller asks himself why his many missed sales, he implements two possible attitudes:

a) or you are puzzled by formulating wrong hypotheses, and you let yourself go to endless mental saws, ("I don't understand them, I offer them an excellent service and what do they do? They MUST THINK! They must think about it! But think about what?", " THEY DON'T HAVE TIME, THEY WANT BUT NOT THE RIGHT

TIME !!! But what do they have to think about ??? I would have bought it!, I would have put trust in someone like me! ", And other similar phrases ..);

b) either a hand is passed over the conscience, and it acts But acts seriously.

As the Neuro Linguistic Programming teaches, one must never, and never, ever move away from the main problem which, in this case, is simple: if a seller has not sold is because I have not been able to do it (first of all), secondly it is because did not target its specific target.
He must always know where to turn, he has to know where to do it, he has to know how and when he needs to know.

We always remember that:

• Every word we say produces a positive or negative effect, in both cases it has consequences.

• Every gesture we show produces a positive or negative effect, in both cases it has consequences.

We come to the focal point of our speech:

• We must always remember that both verbal communication (the word) and non-verbal communication (gestures, expressions) produce a positive or negative effect, for better or for worse; and that every customer is not us and we are not them. Everyone lives their own personal reality made up of subjective desires, subjective ambitions, subjective needs, subjective expectations that remain limited to the sphere of the self.

Once the change has taken place in you, you will only have to understand the right way to deal with the customer so that your spoken words will have the desired effect, in this case we talk about a purchase.

You will be able to make your service or product unique only when your words have made it so; and they will not be the same ones you will pronounce with everyone! No! You will need to be able to change them, adapt them, depending on who you are dealing with. Whether we want it or not, this is the only reality that the seller has to deal with.

=> *We get based on what we give.*

If you want to take flight, you need to know this. And you have to accept it.
If you have already accepted it, you can continue on your growth path to emerge as a true professional in the sector. The Neuro Linguistic Programming applied to the field of sales will allow you, gradually, to understand what will be the best linguistic approach to use in front of what is today an increasingly segmented, increasingly individualized, increasingly privatized working reality.

Bringing the desired object towards itself is difficult, I know, and it is certainly not a sequence of improvised and / or random acts; and it's definitely not child's play. For this a method is necessary (after all, as in all things).
That's why you're reading this book now.

The Oxford English Dictionary describes NLP as: a model of interpersonal communication that mainly deals with the relationship between successful behavior patterns and subjective experiences (in particular the thought patterns) that underlie them.

NLP is, (always referring to the description given by the Oxford English Dictionary), as an alternative therapy system based on this that seeks to instruct people to self-awareness and effective communication, and to change their mental behavior patterns and emotional. The main objective that led to the emergence of Neuro Linguistic Programming was to invent a methodology able to identify ways to help people have better, more complete and richer lives.
For this you are choosing NLP.

During a public conference, about the PNL acronym, Bandler explains that:
"The term NLP alludes to a union existing between the mind and its neurological processes (neuro), the language (linguistic) and the behavioral patterns that have been learned with experience (programming)".
Therefore, according to Bandler, these schemes can not only be organized, but can allow anyone who wants it for their own life to fully achieve each individual goal.

Why believe, therefore, in the strength of Neuro Linguistic Programming understood as a system of alternative therapy based on this that seeks to instruct people to self-awareness and effective communication, and not to other therapies? What more can NLP compare with the others?

The answer is always given to us by Bandler (according to his public statements): "The Neuro Linguistic Programming, compared to all other disciplines, starts from the assumption that human beings were (and are) literally programmable".
If everyone can be literally programmable, everyone can succeed in real change. There are no excuses.

"When I started using the term programming people really got angry. They said things like: "You are saying that we are like machines. We are human beings, not robots" - explains Bandler, "What I was really saying was just the opposite. We are the only machine that can be programmed. We are self-programmable. We can set up deliberately designed and automated programs that work by themselves to deal with boring worldly tasks, thus freeing our minds to do other more interesting and creative things. "

Some people really got angry - says Bandler, they didn't understand the importance of Neuro Linguistic Programming. They were convinced that the approach he had towards people was offensive.

Around the 70s, when people started talking seriously about Neuro Linguistic Programming, it was not at all easy to smooth the terrain;

the beliefs and dogmas then, (as we all know), are the "most difficult things to dismantle, or rather to be reprogrammed. Nobody believed Bandler's words; no one could believe that it was really possible to reprogram their language, their mind and that this reprogramming would lead to an improvement (noticeable) of one's own existence if not, indeed, to a reversal of this.

Still, Bandler didn't give up. During each conference, wherever he attended he did not miss the opportunity to reaffirm the concept on which he had founded the Neuro Linguistic Programming; "we can free our minds - he said - to do other more interesting and creative things.
We can set up deliberately designed and automated programs that work alone to deal with tedious earthly tasks. "

Clear the mind and focus on the creative - this was important, according to Bandler. In one of his books he writes that:

"The thought of Neuro Linguistic Programming is based on the principle according to which each individual is able to create his own perception of the world, and this perception is born from the interaction of his gestures, his thoughts and his words. But the vision of the world (what I call the mind map) can be modified at any time in order to be able to enhance (and improve) both one's own work performance and work perceptions ".

At this point, reflecting on what has been said so far, we understand the importance that can come to us as we approach the world of Neuro Linguistic Reprogramming if we really want our lives to change.
Why? Because most of the time we are absolutely not aware of being (ourselves) the only ones to hinder our growth; we do not realize that we are the ones who impose limits on ourselves and, thus continuing, we create problems, sometimes non-existent.
We sabotage our lives, unknowingly or consciously.
It is a bitter truth: we are the only saboteurs of our life.

Let us take the case in which we did so with full awareness, that we really realized how much damage we do but that we didn't decide to do anything to improve our condition. Let's imagine: we know our limits, we recognize them in the circumstances of everyday life, (sometimes we hate them too), but we continue to always make the same mistakes. Why do we do it? Why are we masochists? Maybe that's right.

When we realize that we do not take advantage of the way we set ourselves and the language we use and do not act to bring about a real change in our lives, then we are true masochists and we have no love for our person.
Recognizing the need for a better transformation in life is the greatest expression of love that we can manifest towards ourselves.

I am reminded of a phrase I want to share with you, which I think can make you think: "Not even your worst enemy can hurt you more than your thoughts can" - Buddha.

That's exactly how it is. However, unfortunately, to understand it we must first hurt ourselves, fall and learn on our skin what it means to take a blow in the face. And then (maybe) we change.
Alas, in all this there is a great truth and it is that you do not run away from the pain caused by the error, you are forced to pass inevitably through this to improve (it may also be that you, who are reading, are beginners and "I have chosen to buy this book simply because you want to learn even before you seriously start your profession. Here, in this case, you were the smartest of us all, because you understood, before me in the first place, how to do it in life).

How many times, in the course of our lives, we have blamed ourselves for the mistakes we made: a missed work contract, a broken relationship due to many misunderstandings or, why not, a common and trivial quarrel. And yes, in many situations we are guilty, because the truth is that every person tends (in hindsight) to rethink (to the nth degree) what he could have said or done in a certain context and that instead, for unconsciousness / inexperience / and so on, did not say or do.
A gunshot and we're off !!! Way to the mental saws: "But how could I have answered that way?", "How did I not convince him? I was one

step away from the closure of that contract! I didn't have to say what I said ...", "It is only my fault if I find myself in this situation now! "," Why do I behave like this? Why should I hurt myself unnecessarily? I should learn to love myself! Maybe you will know how to behave! I can do nothing but harm myself " rationality, if only I could control the strength of my thoughts "," If only you were different ".

"If only you were different".
This sentence, in its simplicity, is the most common reason that pushes any person to approach the Neuro Linguistic Program (just like it happened to me): one gets there to change, to improve, to be free from those patterns it is constructed (the so-called paradigms) that lead us to always make the same mistakes (in speaking, in asking, in acting, in communicating, etc ...).

Always remember that: if we cannot be what we would like to be, it is only because (many times) we are the worst enemy of ourselves. For you who read, let us therefore make this happen no more.
We CAN (if we WANT) make profound changes to our lives and achieve the success that we believe we deserve only at the very moment we acquire the awareness of wanting to make a real change, and to do so, we must apply a method.

We cannot improvise, we would fail regardless. But we can learn thanks to NLP how to apply specific techniques that teach us to modify all those behaviors that damage us to develop, instead, successful reactions.

You have understood that (and I rewrite it so that you can memorize it better):

You have to go beyond your limits, enter into a relationship with those who are listening to you (in this case, your target audience) on tiptoe, slip into their minds to stay out of it. With the necessary precautions, it is obvious. If you are here it is because you want and you have to learn how to do it.

No more words wrong and out of place.

No more unpleasant and disabling gestures / behaviors.
You are ready to learn what to say and when to say it, what to do and when to do it, because Neuro Linguistic Programming (as repeatedly stated) does not accept an assertion: it is not the customer who has not understood, it is you who is not well explained to you .

You must know the words placed within that finite set from which you can draw to be able to improve (no more "if I were you", "trust me", "don't think about it long", and so on).
It is necessary to always be prepared, my friend, it is an invincible method in order not to lose, to make as little mistakes as possible, to reduce the probability of risk.

Don't worry if you are currently in the grip of anxiety and confusion! There is! I know you are wondering how you will learn all these techniques concerning the correct language to use and the right behavior to have with your customers, in a time frame that does not tend to infinity.

I can assure you that once you have learned the ABC of Neuro Linguistic Programming, everything will start rotating in the opposite direction and favorably. If starting tomorrow you will begin to concentrate, and you will begin to eliminate from your vocabulary those brief uncomfortable phrases (which I mentioned in the previous paragraphs; if you don't remember them I would urge you to read them again) trust that something will change in your work.

And then, of course, you will have to continue to study what are the correct words to apply to your sales sector; study learning from books and lessons from your daily experience, be concerned about dedicating yourself to continuous updating by taking training courses; follow the lectures dealing with Neuro Linguistic Programming, informed about new working hypotheses.

What I can advise you is this: you must never stop, you must always find a way to stay on the piece. You'll see that riding the wave won't be difficult for you, then the problem will be to stay (with both feet) afloat. Always put your head on it.

Let's say you finish reading this book (I hope in the blink of an eye) and that, starting tomorrow, you decide to apply these little tips I have given you so far; imagine that the first week of work does not go as you hoped it would.

I would then invite you to reflect on the possibility of proceeding following your model. Many do it, at least in a first phase and, as already written several times, in this you have full support from the Neuro Linguistic Programming.

It is normal that immediately the approach to change will seem difficult to you, it will take some time before you succeed in this long process of transformation, ("too much to know, too much to improve, too much to think about ourselves and ourselves our attitudes, too much to understand..."). Then follow, before starting, this (now mentioned several times) advice that is given to you directly by Neuro Linguistic Programming: the heart of NLP is, in fact, modeling.

Choose your model now.

But don't postpone this research until tomorrow.

It is important that you can find it and feel it similar to you, to your desires for growth; It is important that you are able to reflect your life goals in him.

Also stop reading if you prefer, I don't get offended, the important thing is that you stop now, right now, and identify your character, the one that represents for you the maximum of genius, what for you is the supreme representation of what you hope to be (in every way) in life. Observe his movements, his gestures, his way of speaking; buy (if he has written) his books or follow him on Social Media studying the behavioral approach, both in private and working life; imagine being him and doing what he would do.

But why is it so important to choose a successful model to refer to both at the beginning of our training and during?

It is important because it will allow you, right now, to point to something concrete and not to an abstract ideal; will allow you to aspire to that something that this ordinary person has managed to achieve, while you are still imagining it. So in him you can find a point of reference that encourages you to believe it and that leads you to say "I can do it just like he did before me".

Modeling or "modeling" has been considered (precisely for this reason) the real root of Neuro Linguistic Programming: modeling strategies of thoughts and behaviors of "successful" people to achieve results in life.

The basic concept is this: model how excellent people think for us, then make those thought patterns their own, observing others who have already achieved and live the results we would like to achieve, constantly stimulating our mind towards a direction that can favor the achievement of professional goals.

According to Bandler's statements about modeling, according to the NLP - "modeling" means to directly or indirectly learn the behaviors, attitudes and thought patterns of others. It means copying the structure, the attitude, the thoughts, the beliefs, the questions, the physiology of those who have what others want to achieve. You can model a sporting activity, a work performance, an emotional state.

We can make a distinction between wanted modeling and indirect modeling:

a) indirect modeling, is what distinguishes the attitude of children who imitate (exactly) the actions and attitudes of the greatest.
Children observe the world and have, towards this, a completely unconscious and indirect approach because they learn from outsiders, from third parties. This is because on the part of the child there is no awareness and / or trace of rationality; in simple terms, a child does not choose to imitate his parents' behavior, he does it because for them, they are simply examples to follow (for this reason it is necessary to pay close attention when you are in the presence of a child because, he, is able to absorb any behavior or form of language in the first years of development).
b) The type of modeling towards which the Neuro Linguistic Programming pushes us is what we could define analytic, or better yet conscious and direct modeling, it is in practice a form of modeling wanted. We want to imitate and consciously choose to collect information on the subject we wish to imitate in attitudes,

idioms, use of language, behavior in public; the ultimate goal is to (hopefully) get a result that comes as close to him as possible.

Obviously to create a certain resemblance it is absolutely not possible to try random formulas of improvisation but it is essential to study strategies and techniques that allow it; this requires time, commitment, precision and a lot of awareness. It is the latter that makes the difference between those who make it and who doesn't, you know?

The phrase (which is often said, among other things) is valid: "if he succeeded, I can do it too!". Of course! Of course you can do it! But if you want to do it, then you have to start pointing to him , with awareness you have to start shaping yourself.

At this point in the book you have already acquired most of the theoretical aspects that you missed.
Now you know that:

• There are no magic or tricks that can lead you to immediate success. Success is achieved over time, with energy and a lot of determination.

• Achieving success is possible and it is nothing damn unattainable.

• How you will move, what you will say, in the face of each of your individual customers will.

• We can change the meanings, at any time we wish, through a transformation of the perceptive structure.

• We can model strategies of thoughts and behaviors of "successful" people to achieve results in life.

• That modeling is important because it will allow you, right now, to aim for something concrete and not an abstract ideal; will allow you to aspire to that something that this ordinary person has managed to achieve, while you are still imagining it. So in him you can find a point of reference that encourages you to believe it and that leads you to say "I can do it just like he did before me".

In the previous paragraphs, we have mentioned three elements that I consider indispensable for your professional growth and to these, I would now add a fourth.
Let's review them together:

1. The conviction ("What I do is help people develop the conviction of being splendid people, because when you start to believe it, you also begin to behave accordingly: it is then that you begin to gather fantastic results" - Bandler).

2. Optimism ("It is important to learn to harness the great power of the mind to turn our thoughts into reality, being optimistic is the key to success").

3. The trust towards oneself, towards others, towards one's own change ("You have to believe yourself first in your goals and in your abilities otherwise no success, no sales, no collaborations, no accomplishments; no nothing").

> *you want something you've never had, you have to do something you've never done and you have to do it believing it with all your strength"*
> *(Thomas Jefferson)*

You have to be a motivated salesman to do it. This fourth feature will be extremely useful.
Motivation allows you to build doors that you didn't know you could build; it is the engine of change. Because you know, if you are not motivated, you will never go anywhere; and even if the road will be (very) often tortuous, no matter how long it takes to arrive, what matters is to arrive, for better or for worse.

> *- Luke Skywalker: Well I'll try it!*
> *- Yoda: No! Don't try it. You do it or you don't. There is no proof!*
> *(From the movie Star Wars)*

You cannot attempt change: you must desire it! You must believe it real and possible!

You can start from what you are today to build what you want to become; always do it step by step, do not rush. Haste does not bring good results.

As Sally Berger said: "The secret to moving forward is to start". You'll have to start somewhere. And if you're reading this book it's because you've already started!

Now, please, don't give up and move on! I can only advise you to invest in yourself, because it is the only investment that pays the highest interest.

According to the Neuro Linguistic Programming motivation is one of the main elements in people's lives, and it is all that makes the difference. Therefore, find the motivation in yourself, first and foremost, look at your model and find inspiration in it; let yourself be guided and when you are in a moment of despair, look at it again and admire it to start imitating it in an ever more conscious way.

From your life model you draw inspiration day after day; but the real one, the one you know is the best inspiration for you. Remember:

"The dictionary is the only place where the word success comes before the word sweat" - said Vince Lombardi. So roll up your sleeves and start sweating.

I titled this paragraph "Aphorisms of Bandler, and much more ..." because, in addition to drawing from his explanations about Neuro Linguistic Programming (retouching the principles around which NLP is founded), I consider it important that you can investigate further your studies by referring to the words that Bandler himself published or pronounced in one of his numerous conferences, so that you can make them your own in this process of change and find a profound inspiration, which I sincerely wish you.

At this point you just have to believe it:

• "The problems are non-existent in the absence of the human beings to which they are connected. They do not have a existence of their own in the universe. They exist only in our perceptions and in our giving a meaning to things".

• "Usually, people tend to underestimate man's need to stop from time to time to smell the flowers that grow along that path that is life. All their energy, all their projects are aimed at achieving the result, so there is no room for the path ... Life should be lived as a process, and not as a sequence of material results ".

• "If you believe with every fiber of your being that there is a way, you will probably find it".

• "A typically Western saying is: I will believe it when I see it. We should consider the idea of reformulating it in these terms: I will see it when I believe it. It would be much more accurate and would take into account the fact that the human brain likes images. In fact, as far as we know, it succeeds and gives meaning to the world only through images ".

• "You cannot convince people that what they are experiencing is not the truth. They are trapped inside them precisely because they perceive it as real".

• "Pay very little attention to what the person says he does and a great deal of attention to what he does".

• "People add or subtract information to create their own models of the world based on their own filters ... We experience what we expect to experience, we hear what we expect to hear and, above all, we see what we expect to see".

• "I shouldn't be able to influence your life, you shouldn't be able to influence mine, except by mutual consent, or when you set a good example and prove something".

• "GOOD people get better results in virtually every area of life, compared to their pessimistic counterparts. It is not about being fooled by false hopes, nor denying the reality of the facts. It is about encouraging the belief that things can to improve: the result is that, almost always, they will do it ... Does it mean that all your problems will be solved with a magic wand? Not necessarily: what matters is the BELIEF that every situation, although negative, CAN IMPROVE in a way or another. It is one of the distinctive signs of those who know how to live Happy. "

• "Life should be lived as a process, and not as a sequence of material results".

• "The conviction that it is possible to do it is fundamental so that you can allow yourself to do the necessary actions to do it".

• "If you want to pay tribute to someone, push yourself farther than he did."
"Some things could go wrong. Others might work. You can find both of them out there. If you look for things that could go wrong, you find them. You simply looked at the wrong pile! Look for what works - you'll find that too."

And do you really believe it?

5. The 22 immutable laws of Marketing

"Never write an ad that you don't want your family to read.
If you don't tell your wife, you can't lie to mine. "
(David Ogilvy)

5.1 Hunter Marketing and Attraction Marketing.

"Making promises and keeping them is a nice way to build a brand"
(Seth Godi)
If you are reading this book it is because you want to become one-of-a-kind sellers: self-confident, able to cope with every difficulty, prepared and sure to act with marked determination in professional life and, why not, private life.

We now know that Neuro Linguistic Programming is a discipline that is able to modify every aspect of one's life and that, once you get closer to it, it will be inevitable that everything changes for the better!

It will improve your work performance and you will be able to highlight your strong qualities, the same ones that you did not think you had before even approaching the world of NLP.
All this because you will have rediscovered yourself ... You will have made yourself clear inside you and you will have learned to exalt your qualities rather than obscure them because of your own behaviors, most of the times negative.

The Neuro Linguistic Programming gives you the right stimulus towards change: it is not a simple discipline that you study and this learning remains, then, an end in itself. No! NLP becomes part of the mechanisms of your daily life, without giving up for a moment.

Thanks to Neuro Linguistic Programming you will always be in constant search of stimuli and, the more your approach to work will be positive, and the more positive, in turn, will come looking for you.

Just want it. Free from the mental conditionings that you yourself have created in the course of your existence you will turn your gaze towards new, better horizons, towards infinite horizons.

Your human side will change (if you are a bit of a grumpy person, I hope you will not be offended by hearing this little word, try smiling a little more and you will see what immediate benefits your mood will bring!); as well as your professional side will change (remember: positivity attracts positivity, negativity attracts negativity).

You will know how to juggle yourself with passion in the vast panorama of the world of the market, looking with courage, determination, cunning and strength of mind to always remain afloat.

We have focused a great deal on the aspect of Neuro Linguistic Programming based on personal change, on the ability to modify the mental and linguistic structures that characterize "one's own reality", the intimately private, subjective sphere of each individual.

Now, however, let's move on to an equally important topic so that you can learn how to move within your sector (in full autonomy) and perform your job to the fullest

Because if it is true that personal change will not be long in coming, we need to know exactly which reality we are moving towards.

For this I would like you, now, after learning the basics of Neuro Linguistic Programming, to learn (well) some rules of Marketing.

For what reason? But it's obvious! You are a seller and you need to know how it works in your area!

Always remember, however, that Credibility matters in Marketing!

The rules that maneuver the world of the market will be your daily

bread so you will have to know them well. Then...
Highlighter in hand, and ready for ruthless immersion. If your memory falters, I advise you to write them down on a sheet of paper and always take them with you (in the wallet, in the car, in the breast pocket, and when something doesn't convince you, about a proposal or a simple analysis of market ... Down slip of paper, to refresh the memory. You'll see how useful it will be, from here soon).

Good. Before referring to some specific quotes on Marketing, you should know that there are mainly two categories of sellers that operate within this world: we talk about the category of sellers who belong to the world of attraction Marketing and the category of sellers who belong to the world of hunter marketing.

And you, have you ever wondered which of the two you belonged to? If you still haven't the chance to ask yourself, you're always in time to do it and to choose which one to belong to.

The marketer, (the seller), who belongs to the second category is considered as a hunter and his customers (always potential) are seen as prey to reach, to grab just like the lions do with the deer. In this case, at the time of its market analysis, the marketer asks specific questions: "How can I make a new sale immediately?", "To whom should I bet?", "How can I find (find) a new customer immediately? which offer my service (or my product)? "," How can I sell the salable? "," I want more, how to do? ".

This anxiety (let me pass the term), or rather this state of mind that accompanies him slavishly, generates in the seller the (sometimes exaggerated) desire to conclude a deal as quickly as possible, forgetting however that the customer this anxiety perceives; the consequence can be predominantly one: that the client, feeling cornered, with his back to the wall, escapes with all his feet.

As we have seen, the attitude taken by the hunter marketer does not always produce the effects he wants; he develops strategies and sales techniques that are a bit archaic, if we can define them as such, and furthermore (as we have already stressed several times) his intrusive attitudes tend to produce considerable resistance from the potential client.

The latter feels literally hunted by his proposals, he feels suffocated and will tend to defend himself (even if only by producing objections), just as happens in a common hunting scene. It is the game of the parts: of the prey and of the predator.

Therefore, I strongly advise you against choosing the category of sellers that belong to the world of hunter marketing. I would urge you, instead, to tend to the category that belongs to the world of attraction marketing.

=> There is no better way to enter the world of Marketing (and above all to do Marketing) if not by exploiting the natural force of attraction that people have for the things they really need. And I repeat, for the things they really need.

I want to remind you that the fascination or special qualities that attract people to something constitute what exerts all forms of attraction. Attraction can be both a physical form and a psychological form but, in both cases, it has a driving force that can be exhausted, so it is important to learn to manage it to the best of one's ability.

"Your mental attitude gives your entire personality a power of attraction that attracts circumstances, things and people you think of the most!"
(Napoleon Hill)

This quote is a little the red thread conductor of everything; explains perfectly the role that Neuro Linguistic Programming plays in our lives. If you change your mental attitude, everything around you changes; if the attitude is positive you will get, in response so much positivity, differently, things will not go the right way (negativity attracts negativity).

As you can see, if we think about it, we are all part of a whole that finds a logical order within a system; for this reason it is always essential to understand (or at least try) in which direction we tend.

Credibility is not something that is acquired forever. It should be fed every day.
(Fabrizio Saccomani)

Briefly summarizing, to succeed and improve your life:

=> at the basis of everything there must be four conditions: CONVICTION, OPTIMISM, TRUST, MOTIVATION;

=> these four elements above allow us to have a clear vision of who we are, of what we want for our life, of what we want to change radically in us;

=> at this point the programming of the mental schemes is started (but firstly the programming of the verbal and non-verbal language);

=> Change occurs in behavior and language;

=> only Positivity is obtained;

=> Positivity generates the improvement of professional life and private life;

=> this new light of Positivity that invades us produces the strength of ATTRACTION (our customers): we tend towards them and they will tend, from that moment on, towards us.

5.2 Some definitions of Marketing.

With regard to this very rapid theoretical explanation of Marketing, we have highlighted the existence of two categories of sellers acting within their sector, the category of sellers belonging to the world of attraction marketing and the category of sellers that belong to the world of hunter marketing.
But what is meant by Marketing? Let's look at some of the most famous theoretical concepts. Marketing is a discipline, or rather a

branch of the economy that deals with the study and description of a reference market and, in general, deals with the analysis of the interaction between the market and the users of a certain company .

The term Marketing derives from market to which is added the ending of the gerund to indicate its active participation, or the action on the market itself by the companies.
There are several definitions we have today about Marketing. This distinction is determined on the basis of the role the company plays and the positioning objective of a given panorama, which it has in relation to its competitors.

The company thus distinguishes itself in this vast panorama, in relation to the strategic role it decides to play and the positioning it obtains within its specific (competitive) market area.
The main definition of Marketing is given to us by Philip Kotler known to all for being the father of the most recent developments (regarding the subject) following his works published from 1967 to 2009.

Marketing is defined as that social and managerial process aimed at satisfying the needs and requirements through specific processes of creation and exchange of products and values. It is a discipline that stands out for its ability to identify, create and provide greater value in order to satisfy the needs of a reference market, making a profit: delivery of satisfaction at a price.
Basically, three types of Marketing are recognized:

• "analytical Marketing", ie the study of the market, of customers, of competitors and of their own company in relation to their specific socio-cultural context;

• "Strategic Marketing", which is a planning activity, essentially translated by a company in order to obtain, while favoring the customer, its loyalty and collaboration by all market players, always in relation to to his specific • socio-cultural context;

• "Operational Marketing", ie the type of Marketing able to draw, instead, from all those choices that the company puts in place to achieve an objective within a strategy, always in relation to its specific partner context - cultural.

"Marketing: it is the process of production, promotion, distribution (point of sale) and determination of the price of goods, services or ideas in order to establish satisfactory relationships with the customer in a dynamic environment."
(William Pride and O.C. Ferrel and their generic definition of Marketing)

In 1985, the AMA Board gave this definition of Marketing in order to specify its characteristics: "It is the process of planning and executing the conception, pricing, promotion and distribution of ideas, goods and services to create exchanges and satisfy individual and organizational objectives ", (" It is the process of organizing and executing conception, pricing, promotional activities and the distribution of ideas, goods and services to create commercial exchanges and meet the objectives of individuals and organizations ").

This vision is the one that comes closest to the idea that commonly we have of Marketing understood as the process of the distribution of ideas, goods and services to create commercial exchanges and satisfy the objectives of individuals and individual or public organizations.
A similar definition about the Marketing that we find is the following: "Marketing is activity, set of institutions, creating processes, communicating, delivering, and exchanging offerings that have value for customers, clients, partners, and society at large" , ("Marketing is the activity, the set of institutions and processes to create, communicate, offer and exchange offers that have value for consumers, customers, partners, and society in general").
It is the set of activities that aim to influence a consumer choice.

In recent years, Marketing has instead begun to abandon the transactional perspective to focus more on the perspective of relationship marketing. The AMA has further redefined the concept of Marketing in July 2013, after noticing that this discipline is constantly moving towards new horizons.

Thus the description (reformulated) of Marketing is the following: «It is an organizational function and a set of processes aimed at creating, communicating and transmitting a value to customers, and managing relationships with them in a way that benefits the company and to its stakeholders. "

The ultimate goal of Marketing is to create value for the customer and in fact one of its main purposes is to create a brand positioning in the mind of the consumer through brand management techniques.

The latest trends are aimed at the study of experiential marketing that embraces the vision of consumption as an experience in which the buying process merges with perceptive, sensory and emotional stimuli.

Today there is a branch of Marketing called Management which consists of analyzing, planning, implementing and controlling projects aimed at implementing exchanges with target markets to achieve corporate objectives. Above all, it aims to adapt the offer of products or services to the needs and requirements of the target markets and to the effective use of pricing, communication and distribution techniques to inform, motivate and serve the market.

This Managerial Marketing activity can therefore act as an "interface" between the company and the external context (together with the sales, import / export, public relations and other sectors), observing their behavior and controlling, at least in part, the outgoing information flows from the company (wanted or unwanted), and increasing the knowledge coming from outside; these include the weak signals that allow us to understand, possibly in good time, the changes to the market that will take place in the near future.

In addition to Marketing Management, Services Marketing (airlines, hotel chains, etc.) and Institutional Marketing (made by institutions) must also be mentioned.

Of less economic significance is Political Marketing, as well as that which companies reserve for their employees and which is commonly defined, although improperly, as B2E (business to employee, "business to employee") marketing.

What do the different types of marketing mentioned above have in common?
Obviously, customers, students or patients are their common point; each communication strategy is aimed at selling a product, a service or selling both.
Making sure to attract customers and lead them to themselves is the ultimate goal of Marketing; and we know that there are no other ways of interacting except those that respect a law of attraction: attracting new customers to stand is fundamental.

Professional sales requires a method based on effective and persuasive communication, able to satisfy all the conditions necessary to close contracts with customers (new ones) and to keep customers who are already (old).

But let's see more closely who the recipients for whom we create the different marketing strategies?
Marketing can address both consumers, and in this case we talk about B2C Marketing (business to consumer, "from business to consumer"), often referred to as simply Marketing; or, it can turn to the business market, and in this case it is called Industrial Marketing or B2B Marketing (business to business, "from business to business").

In the health sector in the broad sense, the term disease-mongering indicates the use of particular marketing strategies, aimed at the introduction of a therapeutic protocol or new diagnostic / therapeutic procedures or of a drug ready or next to be placed on the market. This through an appropriate awareness campaign aimed at the introduction of non-pathological clinical pictures, to induce the consumer and / or patient to search for a solution to his "alleged" diseases, which make him still suffering, in order to generate new markets of potential patients.

In addition to Marketing Management, Services Marketing (airlines, hotel chains, etc.) and Institutional Marketing (made by institutions) must also be mentioned.

Of less economic significance is Political Marketing, as well as that which companies reserve for their employees and which is commonly defined, although improperly, as B2E (business to employee, "business to employee") marketing.

What are the different types of marketing mentioned above?
Obviously, customers, students or patient are their common point; each communication strategy is aimed at selling a product, a service or selling both.
Making sure to attract customers is the ultimate goal of Marketing; and we know that there are no other ways of interacting except those of the attraction: attracting new customers to stand.

Professional sales requires a method based on effective and persuasive communication, able to satisfy all the conditions necessary to close contracts with customers (new ones) and to keep customers who are already (old).

But let's see what the recipients are for whom we create the different marketing strategies?
Marketing can address both consumers, and in this case talk about B2C Marketing (business to consumer, "from business to consumer"), often referred to as simply Marketing; or, it can turn to the business market, and it is called Industrial Marketing or B2B Marketing (business to business, "from business to business").

The term disease-mongering, the term disease-mongering. To reach the consumer and / or patient to search for a solution to his "alleged" diseases, which make him still suffering, in order to generate new markets of potential patients.

In the health sector in the broad sense, the term disease-mongering indicates the use of particular marketing strategies, aimed at the introduction of a therapeutic protocol or new diagnostic / therapeutic procedures or of a drug ready or next to be placed on the market. This through an appropriate awareness campaign aimed at the introduction of non-pathological clinical pictures, to induce the consumer and / or patient to search for a solution to his "alleged" diseases, which make him still suffering, in order to generate new markets of potential patients.

The subjects that normally benefit from the use of these strategies are the pharmaceutical companies, the doctors and their professional organizations and those of consumers, the objects of these strategies are consumers, particular groups of patients or entire social classes.

The analysis of the competitive position, which every company does, should be spread in the direction of the various functions, but it is often left to traditional Marketing which uses models such as the "5 forces of Porter" (theorized by the American university professor Michael Porter), models analytics such as the matrix of the Boston Consulting Group or the 7S of McKinsey, market research and surveys and market segmentations.

Trying to go into more detail about the recipients to whom we create strategic communication campaigns, we can say that the different businesses may differ in terms of sales because they have:

(a) real estate clients, that is, I am going to the client (here the focus is different, not the business); they are easy to locate (we find them for example in bars, at the hairdresser, etc.), so by doing I sell to specific categories that are easy to reach, it is not necessary to be experts in direct marketing.

I have the category and I know who I am but, I find them as easily as my competitors find them. This is the real disadvantage. Most likely, our real estate customers already have competitive products. Therefore, I must acquire fundamental skills, I must specialize as soon as possible to make the best use of Marketing techniques. I must be able to convince, I must be credible.

(b) Elusive customers, which is difficult to understand who they are. We don't have a precise list of these customers, they can all be our potential customers in an endless ocean of customers. At this point targeting plays a fundamental role!

The target customer: who is he? We create a campaign to reach directly the customers that interest us, that is those that really need us. The focus will be on identifying the target: "I need to know who I need to communicate in a different, persuasive, direct way"; I have to communicate only with target people.

Obviously to communicate I will have to use the feeling of empathy, (developing an empathic sensitivity is not easy at all, it means putting our moods in the background to try to understand those of others in depth.
So even if your client will reveal habits that you don't like, you won't have to judge him but try to put yourself in his shoes!

5.2 The 22 immutable laws of Marketing.

"Credibility is what they say about you
(person, company or product does not matter) when you are absent
".
(Jeff Bezos)

There is a law of attraction and there are laws of Marketing, immutable and unquestionable that if you decide to ignore it will be your risk and your danger. It seems absurd but these rules, if carefully studied, can save your professional career because those who wrote them were inspired by those criteria of rationality and common sense that, in the long run, the market always rewards.

Let's be clear: the market is full of pitfalls, and we know it. And marketing is a very complex subject, often difficult; it is a constantly evolving subject, because society changes rapidly and unpredictably, as is clearly visible to all.

Nowadays companies - from multinationals to small businesses, to family-run businesses - can no longer afford to make mistakes. But is it possible to avoid or at least minimize errors? For over thirty years two authors have studied what works and what doesn't work in the big business world, to the point of deducing some laws, considered today as universal.

Through the analysis of the strategies of large companies - IBM, Coca-Cola, McDonald's, Sony, BMW, Apple, DHL, and others - and the success and failure rate of the new products, these two great characters have developed 22 universally valid principles : from the law of leadership to that of exclusivity, from the law of unpredictability to that of advertising, (to name just a few).

Taking note of the awareness that we can all learn to attract what we want by following specific verbal (and non-verbal) techniques; having taken note of the fact that Neuro Linguistic Programming applied to sales is able to bring significant advantages to your professional life and, finally, having recognized that credibility will be the winning weapon for you, you must now know that universal laws exist from the which you will never be able to escape, if you want to make a serious career.

It is unquestionable that the Marketing follows the strategies carefully planned by the individual leaders of the sector but, you must know, that the same Marketing is planned by them, taking into account these laws that will always be invariable over time (and that you too must remember !).

Al Ries and Jack Trout are the two top marketing experts in the world, (the two have written books that have become cornerstones of Marketing and Business) that starting from the study of successful companies have distilled these famous 22 immutable laws of Marketing; immutable precisely because they are independent of time and of every change / socio-cultural context to which they refer.

The time has come to discover with me what these 22 immutable laws of Marketing are:

1. Leadership.

The world of Marketing is to be considered more a battle of perceptions than products. In fact, one of the theories that distinguishes Marketing from other disciplines is based on the importance of being first in one's sector: "it is better to be first than to be better than others". In short, it is important to be the first to be a good leader.

"Whoever thinks of guiding others and has no one following him is just taking a walk" - wrote John Maxwell. It is so, we must try to be so good at the point of creating behind us a trail of people who are interested in what we do and what we say; we must be so ambitious that others want to imitate us, that they want to be us. And that's exactly what we do with the model we chose at the beginning of this path of change.
At this point, we need to know that, in the world, there are three types of leaders:

a. there are leaders who tell you what to do;

b. there are leaders who let you do what you want;

c. finally, there are the "lean" leaders, "who come to you and help you discover what to do" - John Shook. This is the difference between a leader who is worth and the other who does not apply. "Those who want to be leaders but are not leaders say things. Good leaders explain them.

Even better leaders show them. Great leaders inspire them." There are leaders and leaders, but what will allow you to assert yourself within this panorama (very, very, very competitive) will be your ability to inspire those who follow you: make sure that others are inspired by you and that they draw from your inspirational teachings for their lives, which let themselves be swept away by the force of change and the desire for success.

"The challenge of leadership is the ability to be able to be strong, but not brutal; kind, but not weak; reckless but not overbearing; reflective, but not lazy; humble, but not shy; proud, but not arrogant; gifted with humor ; but without madness "
(Jim Rohn)

But what are the characteristics that distinguish a leader from the masses?

When we talk about leadership there are so many factors to analyze that have to do with ideas, but also (and above all) with actions. Giving a univocal definition of leader (and leadership) is not at all easy; we can say that leadership is the art of motivating a group of people to act to achieve a common goal.

Being a leader certainly means being able to inspire others (just as I mentioned before) and to always be ready to do so. To do this, there are aspects of one's personality and there are certain characteristics that transform a subject into a director of action. According to Warren Bennis, leadership is "the ability to translate vision into reality".

Specifically, however, what are the skills and characteristics that a true leader must have in order to inspire and motivate others? What do you need to prove, as a good seller, to your customers? What attitude do you have to take in order for them to choose you, and not one of your Competitors?

See, I dwell a little more on this little paragraph because I want you to understand the importance of your way of ports. It is not a trivial concept, it is that something that makes the difference. It is not a joke or a topic to be taken seriously. You must feel yourself to be a true leader in your profession, and you must demonstrate it daily, without excuses.

"What is credibility? Credibility is the probability of being believed".
(Guido Gili)

Keep these adjectives in mind when you try to describe yourself:

=> **POSITIVE!**
=> **RELIABLE!**
=> **SECURE YOU!**
=> **CREDIBLE!**

Leadership is not synonymous with management: these two concepts are not synonyms at all.

A good manager is not necessarily a leader, in fact managers manage to manage projects / clients / clients, monitor the progress of the work, coordinate the team, solve problems, hire staff, sometimes lay off. We can say that the real difference between a manager and a leader is that: managers manage things but leaders lead people. And one does not become a leader by seniority but, exclusively, by skill.

That a company has been in a company for longer or has more experience than a new employee does not mean anything at all, but this does not mean that the manager has the right to become a leader in his field of expertise. One does not become a leader automatically. Senior managers may exist within their own companies, but it is not at all certain that they are leaders and that they know how to manage people.

And again, I want to clarify, that leadership is not having a title: there is no degree that teaches you how to become a leader.

If you want to be a good leader, you must make the most of your potential and those qualities that each of us has: go to refine some specific features and work to improve yourself and your efficiency.

=> HERE BACK TO ENTER INTO GAME THE NEURO LINGUISTIC PROGRAMMING: make the most of your potential and those qualities that each of us has and smooth out those aspects that characterize your behavior or your language that damage you.

What invites you to reprogram NLP in this case? Surely it spurs you to be:

=> **POSITIVE!**
=> **RELIABLE!**
=> **SECURE YOU!**
=> **CREDIBLE!**

Neuro Linguistic Programming gave us the hope of being able to change; now, we know that we must (first of all) be positive, reliable, self-confident and credible sellers. But if we want to become true leaders in the sales sector, specifically, what language and behavioral techniques should we use to be?

As a good leader:

=> you must be able to explain in a clear and concise way to the SMART employees / customers objectives and / or organizational needs of any entity. Don't go long, people don't always have a maximum concentration threshold.

=> Leaders must master all forms of communication, including individual conversations with customers (and others) as well as communications by phone, e-mail and social media. It is you who knows what they want and how to please them, not filter the talks with them by entering third parties; make sure you always reassure them about your presence at any time.

=> Leaders must be able to manage communication between themselves and their staff or team members, "either through an" open door "policy or regular conversations with workers".

=> We have repeatedly mentioned positivity. A customer feels reassured at the sight of an optimistic salesman, ready to appear empathetic in the event that they were needed; you must be a charismatic salesman always ready with a joke. In this way, a serene relationship is established between you and your client, from which excellent working advantages can be obtained.

=> Show off your creativity, your creativity. The leader often finds himself in the situation of having to deal with sudden (unexpected) customer requests for which having a prompt / clear / unambiguous response becomes difficult. In these situations, the good salesman should not let his difficulty be revealed (never touch the hair, the nose! They are typical signs of embarrassment!) Of management but, on the contrary, he must show off his creativity and thinking (at 360 °) how to solve it. There is not always a linear answer to everything, so you will have to show off your inspiration!

=> You must be flexible. Even if I know that sometimes it will seem really difficult.

=> You must be a reliable person. Being reliable is the trump card for being a leader; you have to be convincing, attract the customer towards you and make sure that if you fall in love (in a sense), you must be a valid reason that incentives to buy to understand each other! Customers must be able to feel comfortable communicating their concerns, posing doubts about what they want to buy. If you are not a reliable person and do not enjoy that reputation, it will be useless.

"I always tell people who are entitled to get answers to every question they have. This does not mean that they will like the answers. But I will be sincere and I know they can face the truth, which could create further questions, but we will overcome them " (Ray Davis, CEO of Umpqua Bank)

Your intellectual honesty and your moral integrity are essential characteristics to make others choose you first! Remember: "it is better to be first than to be better than others".

We continue with our list about the 22 immutable laws of Marketing:

2. The Category. If you can't be the first in a specific category, then all you have to do is invent one! Yes, that's right! Invent one! Try to appear as specialized as possible in what you do because people love specialization and, consequently, they will perceive you as the most suitable, among all, to their needs. We must dominate the category we invent and seriously think about which category we can be first!

3. The Mind. Being first in the mind of one of our potential customers is extremely important; it is more important to be in their mind than to be the first on the market; not always who is first has the right to be the best, as we have seen, in this profession, multiple qualities come into play mixed with the ability to know how to sell and to know how to position oneself within one's own reference

market.

4. Perception. Marketing is a battle of perception, as we have said before, not of products. Let's take an example. The objective quality of the product does not count but the perception of this is had. I repeat, many times it is not the quality of the product that finds space in the mind of the purchaser, but it is the perception that the customer has at the time of purchase. Take, for example, Nutella and let's compare it with any other spreadable cream; it is not said that Nutella is more good, exquisite spreadable creams exist, yet an idea is created in people's minds. And that idea is difficult to get away from it or have it replaced by another. In marketing, perception is a fundamental word because it is the first point on which you should base your entire communication strategy! "Perception is the psychic process that operates the synthesis of sensory data in meaningful forms".

5. Focusing is the most powerful concept in the world of marketing. If you can teach your market segment the association between your product and a single word, a single benefit, you will be the leader of that market! Focusing allows you to be the specialist in the category, allowing you to get rid of the competition. I repeat: Marketing is owning a word in the mind of our potential customer, if you teach the market segment the association between your product and a single word, you will be the leader of that market (for example, in the mind of the customer the Brand Mercedes is synonymous with elegance, safety Volvo, etc.).

6. Exclusivity. It is clear that two companies must play exclusively: their communication strategy must tend to choose specific words that can represent their product (and product quality) in an exclusive way! A fashion brand differs from another in having certain characteristics and, consequently, chooses an exclusive adjective with which to position itself within the market. Two fashion brands cannot use the same word because, in the mind of the customer, this only creates confusion. Remember: two companies cannot have the same word in the mind of the potential customer.

7. La Scala. The strategy to adopt depends on which peg of the scale

you occupy, if we are second to someone, we have to use a different strategy (are we seconds? It doesn't matter, we don't give up and, on the contrary, we create a different marketing strategy, ad hoc, modeling it by transporting it 'optics from negative to positive).

8. Duality. "In the long run every market becomes a two-horse race" (let's take the example of the giants McDonald's vs Burger King, or Hertz vs Avis, etc ...), this means that, even if you manage to be the first in a category, inevitably over time other brands will buy to avoid you from the dominant position, so you have to find a way to enter that reference market and try to make a difference.

9. The Opposite. "If you fight for second place, your strategy is dictated by the leader", or you will have to find strategies that are contrary to the strategies your opponent is using (example: Coca Cola has 100 years of history, Pepsi is for new generations!).

10. The Division. "Marketing can be seen as a sea of ever-expanding categories, there is never an end". The categories are endless, they can develop continuously.

11. The Perspective "The effects of Marketing are felt over a prolonged period of time, the long-term effects are often contrary to the short-term ones" (for example, the sales strategy, that is, if I get them used to them) to buy at a lower price I will probably earn more then, but through my commercial policies I will get them used to buying from me only with the sales). So be patient at the beginning and then enjoy the effects in the future!

12. The Extension. "There is an irresistible pressure to extend the heritage of a brand", when you try to be everything to everyone you end up INEVITABLY in trouble (an example is the fish restaurant that proposes, within the Menu, pizzas to please everyone). If you want to be everything, you risk becoming nothing. Better to be strong in something weak in everything!

13. The Sacrifice. "We have to give up something to have something": to sacrifice are the products (we must restrict our field

and be specialized), the target (useless to want to be everything for everyone) and the changes (only what doesn't work changes, not everything).

14. The Attributes. "For each attribute there is an opposite and effective" (we always take the example of Coca Cola which indicates tradition and Pepsi which indicates, instead, the New Generation, are antithetical concepts that serve much to distinguish from the point of view of Marketing).

15. Sincerity. "If you admit a negative quality, the potential customer will recognize a positive one." One of the most effective ways to get into the head of the potential customer is to first admit a negative fact and then turn it into a positive one. Nothing is more complicated than sincerity.

16. The Singularity. "In every situation only one move produces substantial results". You can do many Marketing actions but it will only be a specific action that will make the difference. Marketing is a war, leveraging the Competitor's weak point is the strategic and effective move that will give you the turning point.

17. Unpredictability. "Unless you write your competitors' plans you can't predict the future," you can't predict what products or services will launch them on the market or you can shape your strategy on their own.
18. Success. "Leads to arragonza and arrogance to failure", this happens when a company has had many successes and therefore of merits and, often, it is convinced to be able to know more about the market itself, to know exactly what people want, instead, they are the starting point.

19. The Bankruptcy. "Failure must be taken into account and accepted", the goal is to limit losses and accept that it could occur.

20. The advertising frame. "The situation is often contrary to what appears in the press."

21. Acceleration. "Successful programs are not built on temporary

fashions but are built on market trends", this is because they have perseverance.

22. Resources. "Without adequate funding, an idea cannot take off" because Marketing is a struggle and this we must always remember, so those with more resources win and apply in all the Marketing process.

6. THE RIGHT WORDS TO SELL

*"Worse than those who lie in words
there is only one who loses credibility with behavior ".*
(Anonymous)

6.1 Remember that ...!

In the second volume of the collection on Neuro Linguistic Programming applied to sales you will find listed all the correct words with which to create your strategic communication and all the harmful words to be banned (categorically) from your vocabulary.

You will find useful tips to get in touch with your potential customer; now that you're halfway through your eye not to give up. You have learned essential notions up to now (forgive me if at times I have had to, by force of circumstances, repeat sentences and concepts or if I have been boring with theoretical quotations but it was useful for you) that will throw, right now, new bases on which your career.

In the next book you will discover (in detail) the technical words to use and the right behaviors to have in order to become a real sales professional, you will find practical and easy to remember examples.

You gave away your training path.
From tomorrow you will begin to analyze what your customers say and to guess what they think.
To do this, remember that you must observe what he tells you with words and what he tells you with body language. Perhaps you might think that very extroverted people can tell you everything you need to hear about your sales business, but you should always keep in mind that many times, even people themselves cannot understand what they really want, they are not able to understand what They wish.

For this reason a good salesman must be able not only to understand the explicit needs of the customer but, above all, the implicit ones.

Let the other person feel free to express themselves. Remember that in that moment there are two different worlds that try to talk, so being able to find compromises is an indispensable quality for those who want to become a good salesman.

Always make your client feel involved. The customer must be involved in the sales process and you must persuade him that his opinion matters, it is extremely important.
Always value your customers even when you are in complete disagreement about their way of living life and their behavior. Remember that your goal is to make the sale so you should not be interested in what your customer does in life!

Recognize emotions and enhance them. The sales techniques manage to have a strong impact on the life of the customers if they can make them feel emotions. The emotional component is very important in sales, I play an essential role, so don't think that the sale is just something material you are proposing and your customer buys: you have to create a relationship base.
When a customer expresses his emotions, his fears, his disinterest related to specific perplexities, you must try to understand them and value them so that they are oriented towards selling the product.

So listen to it but answer it right. Recognizing emotions also means recognizing their legitimacy, giving it value: the customer will recognize this act of kindness. Avoid contradicting him.

As you will learn from the second volume, there is a specific body language, made up of small gestures, useful for hitting the client. Sometimes, for example, a handful or even a gift is enough, which some sellers do to thank their customers for trust, to make a difference.
These small gestures contribute to making the customer feel important, and when a person feels this way, he will try to do something that is worthy of the importance paid to him.

If problems arise, apply all your creativity and flair to solve them; make your customer feel safe with you. Always remember that the important thing is never to break down and propose alternative solutions; show skill in problem solving, be confident and positive.

In some cases you will be allowed to talk about yourself, but not always !!! Sometimes to tell the customer important episodes of our life can be, for them, a source of inspiration, or it can also be, for them, very rewarding as you will have given the impression of trusting his listening skills: you put your trust in him just like he does with you. Also in this circumstance the customer will feel it is important for you, he will feel satisfied and will tend to do something up to the importance given to him.

Remember never to judge who ever you are! Don't assume self-centered, picky, arrogant attitudes. Be patient, optimistic and engaging. I offer them your differentiating value!
Focus on your skills.
Make them understand who the best is, and be credible. Get them to say, "I want him!"

In the next volume I will also explain how to improve the acquisition of your target audience, the meaning of terms such as: lead page, squeeze page, capture-name page, lead magnet, landing page and funnel. Because even if your client does not have the slightest idea what they mean because he is not in, like you, in network marketing, it is good that you know them to have a complete and highly professional training.
And again words like: prospecting, recruitment, sponsorship, downline and upline, etc.

"What is credibility? How can one be credible? Undoubtedly credibility refers to the possibility of being believed. The problem of credibility in communication and, in general, in human relations, is very crucial and actual. Practically not there is a realm of social life in which the problem of credibility does not come into play, starting from the parent-child relationship, to educational communication, to the information system or to political activity.Everyone wants to be credible, but the projected credibility does not match always as much

perceived credibility ".
(Rosalba Miceli)

If you want to be credible you need to know what you do.
Therefore it will be very important to define the "Before" status of
your ideal client and choose a targeted target that can be really
useful. Doing Follow up must be your main focus: when you impact
with a client, it is not necessarily the right condition for there to be a
real possibility of synchronization between you and him (despite
being willing to do so or willing to do so).

Probably at that moment you are not a priority for him, this is the
real clash of the sales world. And you have to know this before you
start.
Once you have defined the Before status, you will move on to
defining the "After" status of your ideal client. The after, or what
you do after meeting him, after concluding the negotiation. There is
a before, there is a during, but there is also an after.
But of the before, during and after we will talk about it in detail in
the next book soon out.
I strongly advise you to do a detailed analysis before entering into a
relationship with your client. ask yourself:

=> *What are your wishes or goals in life?*
=> *What are you trying to accomplish when I interpose with him?*
=> *What do you really need?*
=> *What do you want to experience?*
=> *Who wants to be?*
=> *Am I adding value to his life?*

Remember to define every objection your client might make to you
!!!
The reasons why you might decide NOT to buy your product or
service could be endless. Why would anyone decide NOT to buy
from YOU? Are you credible enough? Do you have the right
experience to guarantee your skills?

And most importantly, have you built a relationship of trust with him

??? He might not even know you at all, not knowing anything about you.

Other objections, in general, are also reduced to the customer's lack of time and money so try to fully understand why this customer does not really want you !!!

Now you will need to invest some time to define your client's appearance. To do this, you will have to "immerse yourself" in his mind.

Let us ask "What does our ideal client really want", "What could his will be?", "What do you want to accomplish?"; and when you understand it try to tune into it by imagining a conversation with his mind.

"You have to get exactly where your ideal client is, not where you think he should be."

Try to understand where he is looking for solutions to his problems or concerns, where he spends his time online and offline, which events he takes part in. What do you like doing in your private life, what blogs follow, what events interest you.

Try to take it to you. Try to be the most credible of all.

Our reading time together for the moment stops here.

I like to greet you (with the hope of finding you again at the next exit), once again remembering the issue of credibility because, as you may have noticed, it is extremely important.

Not only for Neuro Linguistic Programming, for Marketing (of whatever nature it is), but for the life of each person and for his professional success is an essential element.

If you are credible everyone will listen to you, observe you, admire you.

If you are credible you even risk winning, you know?

"Credibility can be based on three different roots.
The first root is constituted by knowledge and competence, that is by the (recognized) quality of an expert.
His prototype in modern Western culture is the credibility of the scientist, but the credibility based on knowledge is also that of the teacher as an expert in a particular discipline, of the doctor as

capable of "curing" according to the dictates of medical science, of the journalist when carries out its work according to the rules of accuracy, completeness of information, verifiability.
More generally, it is the credibility of the "well informed" person, who reports the facts because he has assisted you or because he has a certain knowledge of it ".

(Guido Gili)

www.ingramcontent.com/pod-product-compliance
Lightning Source LLC
Chambersburg PA
CBHW020558220526
45463CB00006B/2354

* 9 7 8 1 6 5 1 7 5 3 7 4 3 *